HELPING CHILDREN
WITH COMPLEX NEEDS
BOUNCE BACK

of related interest

Help your Child or Teen Get Back On Track
What Parents and Professionals Can Do for Childhood Emotional and Behavioral Problems
Kenneth H. Talan, M.D.
ISBN 978 1 84310 870 2

Children with Complex and Continuing Health Needs
The Experiences of Children, Families and Care Staff
Jaqui Hewitt-Taylor
ISBN 978 1 84310 502 2

Self-Esteem Games for Children
Deborah M. Plummer
Illustrated by Jane Serrurier
ISBN 978 1 84310 424 7

Kids Need...
Parenting Cards for Families and the People who Work With Them
Mark Hamer
ISBN 978 1 84310 524 4

HELPING CHILDREN
WITH COMPLEX NEEDS
BOUNCE BACK

Resilient Therapy™ for Parents and Professionals

KIM AUMANN AND ANGIE HART

Illustrated by Chloe Gerhardt

Jessica Kingsley Publishers
London and Philadelphia

First published in 2009
by Jessica Kingsley Publishers
116 Pentonville Road
London N1 9JB, UK
and
400 Market Street, Suite 400
Philadelphia, PA 19106, USA

www.jkp.com

Library of Congress Cataloging in Publication Data
A CIP catalog record for this book is available from the Library of Congress

British Library Cataloguing in Publication Data
A CIP catalogue record for this book is available from the British Library

ISBN 978 1 84310 948 8

Printed and bound in the United States by
Thomson-Shore, 7300 Joy Road, Dexter, MI 48130

CONTENTS

ACKNOWLEDGEMENTS

Resilient Therapy™ is the innovation of Angie Hart and Derek Blincow with support from Helen Thomas and Kim Aumann. This book attempts to translate their thinking into ideas and matter-of-fact suggestions for parents and professionals to use in everyday ways. Many of the ideas may well be familiar to you because they're used in family support work by different sorts of practitioners. It's hard to know who to accredit what to, as they are the result of a range of experiences including:

- tips and inspiration we have collected over the years from parents who've been at the coalface raising children with a range of special needs, disabilities and complex physical and mental health needs

- absorbing information from conferences, books, research papers and journal articles about building children's resilience

- raising our own children of course, and

- testing various well-established strategies and techniques in our own practice with children, young people and their families.

So it's impossible to acknowledge every source and contributor; however, there are a few people in particular who we wanted to be sure to thank. First, the six parents who so generously helped us trial some of our ideas and approaches: Karin Anjos, Helen Arnold Jenkins, Susan Bradford, Chrysi Brown, Sinead Gillespie and Samantha Selway. They provided rich and amusing comment all throughout the planning and writing of this book, without which one of us would have definitely given up. Second, this book would not have been possible without the financial support given to our research by the Community University Partnership Project (CUPP). Third, thanks to Chloe Gerhardt for careful editing of the final manuscript, helping us find some sources of inspiration and doing the illustrations; Ros Cook from Amaze for commenting so sharply on the drafts; Jane Bradford for helping us with the detail about diet and exercise; Peter Goodall for illustration ideas; and David Secrett for his contribution to the parent workshops and meetings where we tested some of our ideas.

And finally, thanks to each of our families for chipping in and for being so patient with us. Writing this book has certainly given us the opportunity to take a long hard look at our own parenting and notice how challenging it is to translate good ideas and theory into practice. And of course, despite all the fabulous input we've had from so many people, any shortfalls in this book too are ours.

INTRODUCTION

What is resilience?

Chances are you have picked this book off the shelf because you think you'd like your child to be more resilient. Or you might be a practitioner wanting to give parents some tips on how they can help their children. While you may not feel entirely sure about what resilience involves, somewhere in the back of your mind the word echoes thoughts of happy thriving children, coping with the ups and downs of everyday life.

But particularly if you are a parent, chances are you're also feeling a bit worn down as you've probably tried a whole heap of things to help your child, most of which you think have made little difference. Take some comfort right away then. This book is about Resilient Therapy™ (RT) and its starting point is that, no matter what, there is always something that can be done, however small.

You may be wondering, what do they know about what it's like to live with challenging children and deal with their support needs day in day out and stay upbeat? Well, we're in the same boat: between us we face quite a few challenges on that front.

We know from our own experience, and from the experience of parents we've worked with, that it's hard raising children with complex needs. Angie has three adopted children all of whom have a range of special needs. She has also worked for many years with children and their families. And Kim has led the work of a parent-led charity supporting parents of children with disabilities and special educational needs for over 15 years. Our joint experience tells us that bringing up children with complex needs can leave parents feeling miserable, deskilled, bemused and disarmed. Practitioners, as well, often can feel that little they do makes much difference.

So we both know what it can be like to think you've run out of ideas for new things to try, and to feel completely overwhelmed, alone and let's face it, for some of you perhaps, even allergic to your child. Rest assured that we have found RT useful in dealing with our own challenges. So we're not just writing a book about it, we're also living it.

Defining resilience

To begin, let's get to grips with the term 'resilience'. It's quite a tricky word to define. Why? Because despite the research undertaken over the past 30 years it remains difficult to pin down, scholars don't all share the same view, it's hard to measure and the thinking is shifting as we learn more.

Interestingly, when we've run workshops with parents they've come up with a helpful spread of ideas: the ability to cope; long-term strength; capacity to bounce back from challenges or deal with trauma; inner strength that you either have or don't; changeable and different depending on the place and situation; and a skill that's possible to learn. One parent even wondered if it was a military term because she thought it suggested building forces and defences to combat threats. Not too far off the mark, but we bet you find it hard to match these ideas with the following definitions from the theorists. Some of the language is a bit complicated, but have a look at this summary:

Ways of thinking about resilience

- 'A class of phenomena characterised by good outcomes in spite of serious threats to adaptation or development.' (Masten 2001, p.228)

- 'The indication of a process which characterizes a complex social system at a moment in time.' (Fonagy *et al.* 1994, p.233)

- 'Adequate provision of health resources necessary to achieve good outcomes in spite of serious threats to adaptation or development.' (Ungar 2005, p.429)

- 'Ordinary magic.' (Masten 2001)

- 'Resilience does not constitute an individual trait or characteristic... Resilience involves a range of processes that bring together quite diverse mechanisms...' (Rutter 1999, p.135)

- 'Resilience is an emergent property of a hierarchically organized set of protective systems that cumulatively buffer the effects of adversity and can therefore rarely, if ever, be regarded as an intrinsic property of individuals.' (Roisman *et al.* 2002, p.1216)

Don't give up just yet, because this book aims to simplify the language, research and theory to make it work for children and families in real life. We reckon having an understanding of what the researchers are on about should help!

So for starters, you might notice that these definitions don't make it very easy to explain resilience as a quality, something that's inside a person. Rather, for most of the people trying to define it, it's more about a big thing that happens, or a set of smaller things that have a positive chain reaction. To really be true to the ideas that researchers have about resilience, it doesn't make much sense to say that this or that person is or isn't resilient. This might come as a surprise, as in everyday language we do talk about resilient children, making it seem as if you *can* somehow say that one person is resilient and another isn't. The main point we need to make here is that resilience is mostly not about what's inside you, but about the way you respond to life's challenges, or the things that are put in place around you to help.

You might be interested to learn that some researchers think resilience is too vague and general a concept to actually be of much help. They say that if you can't point to it as a quality in children, it doesn't actually exist as a thing in itself, but is rather just a collection of other things, like positive self-esteem, good coping skills and so on. Another point they argue about is, how can you measure resilience if it isn't something you can actually identify?

We understand what the critics are getting at, that resilience is hard to measure, but still we find it very useful as an overall idea in helping children and families improve things. It's a good shorthand. So, just in case you're now feeling more confused, the definition for resilience we use throughout this book goes like this:

> Things that happen, or resources we might put in place, that improve the odds for a child where they are stacked against them. A bit like a rubber ball bouncing back into shape.

We also use the word 'resilient' to illustrate a snapshot of a child in time where the end result of an event or process means they've done better than we would have expected, given the circumstances.

But really, it's not the definition of resilience that we're most concerned about. We're interested in what parents and others can do to help children get more out of life than might be expected, so we're focusing on what we'll call here for now resilient practice. And we really do see parents as doing this too, not just people who get paid as therapists.

The definition of this is:

The kinds of things we need to make happen (e.g. events, parenting strategies, relationships, resources) to help children manage life when it's tough. Plus ways of thinking and acting that we need ourselves if we want to make things better for children.

We talk more about this a little further on in this chapter but, first, let's summarize a bit more about how researchers have thought about resilience.

Research on resilience

Originally, researchers' focus was very much on individual children, identifying characteristics present in those who were managing well, like their temperament and intelligence. But it wasn't long before they also recognized the importance of social factors like family relationships, friends and schooling. What's clear and what researchers agree on is that there is no single resilience trait. Instead, you can often pinpoint particular characteristics, features and circumstances that are consistently present when children do surprisingly well in the face of major difficulties. Have a look at this list:

Resilience traits

- Cheerful temperament
- Conventional good looks
- Intelligence
- Educational success
- Ability to solve problems
- Social skills
- Positive self-esteem
- Positive role models
- Self-control
- Stable and supportive family
- Relationships

No surprises there, but what an irritating list. When we've shown it to parents, some get cross and question the definitions of these factors. Most of the parents we've worked with so far are white British, so we suspect we'd get even more objections if we had worked with a more culturally diverse group of parents. It's worth saying here that the majority of studies on resilience so far haven't looked very closely at differences in race, ethnicity, culture and community.

But even if you accept the definitions, the point is to remember that just because some children don't have a fair share of these traits doesn't mean we can't help them do better in life. So please don't bin this book yet just because you think your child hasn't got many or any of the things mentioned. RT is interested in how we can turn what we know from the resilience research to the advantage of children who don't automatically have a pocket full of these qualities or circumstances. Think back to the definition we use and the idea of a combination of ways of thinking, responses and activities that improves the odds for a child where it seems like they are really stacked against them.

Resilience research in general has started more recently to shift its gaze to what researchers call processes, or mechanisms. These are the sequence of events, the situations put in place around children, and the means they themselves use to improve things. We talked about them earlier on when we gave you our working definition of resilience and resilient practice, but we didn't say too much because we didn't want to overcomplicate things in our first few pages. Each of the following chapters in this book will give you specific examples of what this all means.

Researchers have also got very interested in the role of others in helping children do better than might be expected – this is part of the debate about what they call resilient mechanisms. And the children we're talking about include children with complex needs. And that's where this book comes in. We want to help you to know more about particular mechanisms and processes that can be useful, so that you can put things in place to help your children.

Resilient language

The idea of resilience is complex and the language is tricky. Having introduced you to what the academics say about resilience earlier, let's put some of these ideas into more everyday language that avoids thinking of resilience as being 'in' children. This next list describes some of the ways of thinking and doing that we're trying to promote in this book. We're mentioning them here because we think it's really important not to think of resilience as a specific trait that children either have or not, but instead to think about resilience as something that we're doing and building, as an action that's taking place.

Getting the language a little clearer!

- Making your life work in a more resilient way.
- Bouncing back when things are difficult.
- Doing things resiliently.
- Reflecting on how you manage things resiliently.
- Doing better than you think you would.
- Dealing with difficult things resiliently.
- Putting together resilient approaches, responses and actions.
- Developing resilient activities.
- Thinking in a resilient way.
- Getting used to resilient ways of working.
- Putting a resilient spin on things.
- Sorting a store of resilient resources.
- Building up resilient capital.
- Tackling things resiliently.

They are all action and doing phrases rather than static, immovable ones.

Introducing Resilient Therapy

RT is a new way of thinking about increasing a child's ability to respond resiliently when life is tough. We've found that it can be helpful to think of it visually as a Magic Box full of different potions and remedies from which you can choose what's needed to strengthen a child. Or if you don't like the idea of a Magic Box, think of it as a pick and mix toolkit. Within the Magic Box or toolkit are five 'potion bottles' or compartments: Basics, Belonging, Learning, Coping and Core Self. And within each of these five arenas is a range of possible things to do and try, some borrowed from other therapies and some new ones that we have developed through our own RT practice.

As you approach the task of building your child's capacity to manage the challenges of life, you open the Magic Box or toolkit and consider which potion to use. From here, you have the possibility of drawing from just one or mixing ideas from two or all five to create a new combination to suit your own unique situation. In essence, you begin to think tactically about ways of helping your child, basing what you do on what you already know about your child, what's worked and not worked in the past, what you might have the energy to try, and what they are likely to manage themselves. We explain and illustrate the Magic Box in more detail a little further on. Angie and her colleague Derek Blincow have written another book spelling out the ideas behind RT. It's called *Resilient Therapy: Working with Children and Families* (Hart, Blincow with Thomas 2007). That book is aimed at practitioners but some parents have found it helpful too, so we've listed the details, together with other publications we refer to as we go along, at the end of the book.

So who is this book written for? Well, we've taken a really broad view of 'complex needs'. The children we are mindful of throughout this book are those: with worryingly low self-esteem and flagging confidence; with behaviour problems or physical or mental health needs; at risk of school exclusion; who are socially withdrawn; who are disabled; and who have special educational needs. We decided to use the term 'complex needs' throughout knowing it's not perfect or the preferred term for some but hoping it was a good enough solution to finding a language that most could relate to without isolating too many along the way.

The children we had in mind when we wrote this book are aged somewhere between 5 and 12 years. But when we start talking about children with complex needs, their age doesn't always tell us enough about their developmental level or ability. So we've included a table summarizing the child development stages at the end of this chapter. It's very general (the information is available in more detail on lots of websites and in countless books) but, the point is, it might help you think about how to vary your language and behaviour to match your child's level of understanding and ability. And if it's quite challenging do this, don't forget that chances are you'll know if you're going at a pace they can handle. If they seem comfortable with what you are doing, trust it. Keep in mind that milestones should not become millstones. No two children, and especially children with complex needs, develop in exactly the same way; they gather skills within a certain range and at their own pace.

And we use the term 'parent' throughout in the hope that readers will accept it as a general word to include anyone in a parenting role such as foster and adoptive parents, grandparents and carers too. We expect you'll appreciate the difficulty we have with language and forgive any unintended exclusion.

Practising resilient ways of thinking and acting

Knowing about resilient ways of thinking and acting is the first step towards finding ways to promote it with children. And as you will read in this section, RT provides the chance to select and choose the areas where you concentrate your efforts to do this. It's interested in building on a child's assets and strengths and transforming these to situations where they are struggling.

Have a go at this exercise as it might better explain what we mean. First of all, experiment with an example of your own, then try doing it with your child in mind.

ON THE LOOK OUT...

1. **Find one thing where you respond resiliently, even when there are obstacles. How do you manage to do this?**

   I try to ask my child what they've done at school today even though I'm not that interested. I manage to do it because I reckon it's what a good enough parent is supposed to do.

2. **Now think of any obstacles that get in the way of getting this task done.**

   It's boring, I haven't much time. I'm more interested in what I've been doing in the day. I feel like a broken record. They're hungry and moody. I'm still cross with them from last night. I'm crabby because they haven't got much conversation or vocabulary. They answer in monosyllables.

---

3. **What keeps you on track, even when there are obstacles in the way?**

   (Think for example of your instinctive thoughts, behaviours, coping strategies and basic beliefs that help you manage the situation.)

   I remind myself that part of being a good enough parent is showing some vague interest, even when I'm not. I try to think, they'll be in bed at 10 p.m., and so I'll think about me later. I remind myself that tomorrow's another day, so I put the fact that they deliberately broke my chair yesterday out of my mind. I bend at the knees, and talk into their face, making eye contact and forcing myself to smile.

   (*Now* see if you can find an area of your child's life where they're already doing better than you might think.)

4. **Think of one situation where your child perseveres or keeps on with something even though it's tough. What are the strengths they use in this situation?**

   (It might be at school or at home and it might be a very ordinary everyday task. You're looking to hit upon a situation when they have to be, for example, thoughtful, smart, witty, reflective or inventive to keep on. And remember, it can be as small a step as you like.)

5. **Now think of a few obstacles that get in the way of this situation going smoothly.**

6. **Despite the obstacles, what are the things they do that make them carry on?**

   (Think about how they manage by using, for example, coping strategies and certain behaviours, thoughts, emotions or assumptions.)

Noticing where strengths exist in children provides the chance to transfer these qualities to situations in their life where they are not managing so well. Believe us, there are ways to do this, even for those children who really struggle to transfer learning from one situation to another.

While all children should have the chance of achieving things, our primary interest is in making RT work for those children and families managing the most disadvantages. We know children with complex needs fit this category because, for example, they are frequently living in or on the margins of poverty, are vulnerable to the influences of prejudice and discrimination, are on the receiving end of others' negative attitudes, report disproportionate levels of bullying and are managing the ongoing daily demands of their particular impairment.

However, despite this rather bleak picture, there *are* children living with few assets, limited resources and risky situations that appear hopeless to us, but who have somehow done well despite the obstacles. How has this happened? What is it about these children or the people and situations around them that helps them jump the hurdles? How do we duplicate, package and promote these factors for children who could do with a bit more help? This is where RT comes in. RT is specifically interested in catching the learning from research, combining it with real practice experience and applying it to those children who have the odds stacked against them. It's about learning ways of dealing with difficulties resiliently.

The last few decades have seen a great deal of psychological and therapeutic work with disadvantaged children focusing on the deficits and risk factors at play. While we appreciate there is benefit in knowing how far a child strays from the 'norm' and considering ways to reduce their risk factors, we think it's not always the most helpful way to approach their situations. And it hasn't helped us know what to do to support a child and family cope with the everyday challenges of real life. We think RT provides a different way of thinking about children who are struggling. It counters the 'doom and gloom' as its interest is in finding out what makes children strong rather than weak.

When we say therapy, we're not saying you need to be a qualified therapist to do RT. It's for anybody who wants to make a difference. And we've written this book very intentionally for parents because we think you are perfect candidates to become children's resilient therapists. If this all sounds a bit too much, don't worry because we plan to take you through the ideas of RT step by step. Sometimes it gets forgotten that parents are the full-time practitioners charged with the daily and long-term care of their children.

And of course, the more challenging your child is, the less anyone else wants to look after them. So while we might wish this wasn't the case, the fact is that you get the brunt of it. And to top it all, in our experience the knowledge and skill gathered by professionals doesn't always get translated to parents even though they are best placed to make a real difference for children. Anyway, you probably wouldn't be reading this if you didn't feel up to trying to do things differently.

> **Message for professionals**
>
> This book is written for parents, but if you're a practitioner interested in understanding the unique journey involved in bringing up children with complex needs and you want to strengthen a parent's capacity to manage the difficulties thrown their way, it's for you too. In fact we hope you'll use it with parents. And every time you work with parents, hold in your mind the question, how well would I do if faced with these challenges 24 hours a day?

We think learning the RT approach can help. And we have found that the actual process of doing RT with children can bolster your own resilient abilities too. Lots of parents and professionals tell us that they feel uplifted and energized as a result of building children's ability to bounce back when things are tough.

I had run out of ideas, these were fresh thoughts.

It's really a useful way to come at problems with my kids.

I felt inspired to try again.

The positive approach made me feel better.

We hope you manage to recognize your own experience and expertise as you go about the business of learning more about RT. Whether you're a parent or professional reading this book, we thought you might appreciate these few words of wisdom from Dr Donald Winnicott, who was a renowned paediatrician and child psychoanalyst. His work has profoundly influenced the way we approach supporting children and families today. Apart from introducing the concept of 'good enough parenting' and developing a myriad of helpful ideas, he worked with some of the most disadvantaged children and families with a real humility about the people who spend lots of time in the physical presence of children they find hard to deal with. Here's what he said to a residential staff team working in a youth offenders institution.

A word of wisdom

> I want to make clear…that I know I could not do your job. By temperament I am not fitted for the work you do; and in any case I am not tall enough or big enough. I have certain skills and a certain kind of experience, and it remains to be seen whether there can be some pathway found between the things that I know something about and the work that you are doing. (Winnicott 1958, p.90)

How to use this book

Dip into these pages when the timing is right. Learning any new skill takes time, energy and a big pinch of determination. You'll already know that there are no simple answers and you cannot transform children overnight, so taking a long-term view helps. The same is true of this book. It doesn't need to be read all at once and is designed for you to flick through as and when you've got the energy. Our guess is that some of you will read this from cover to cover. And others will pick it up when things are particularly tough and you're looking for something new to try.

When you're feeling really desperate, remember this time will pass. If at times you can't do anything more than simply write out one of the ideas or thoughts that we have peppered this book with, and pin it up next to your bed, at least you are doing something.

We've included a range of short exercises and worksheets because we had a hunch that they might help make sense of the theory and ideas we're trying to explain. But it's not vital for you to do these to discover more about RT. Do them if you can be bothered, skip over them if you prefer concentrating on the text. We had six parents helping us test the exercises and, not surprisingly, we got six different responses. There aren't any right responses so we haven't printed the answers upside down at the bottom of the page! However you use this book, we hope at the very least it gives you some new ideas to add to your toolkit.

RT should help you, but you wouldn't be the first parent to raise some doubts:

Q&A – WHY SHOULD I BOTHER WITH RT?

Parent: So what's new about RT, it all seems obvious?

RT Parent: It can be hard to know where to begin when children are managing an assortment of difficulties. RT is designed for the most disadvantaged children and families, so unlike some therapies which are designed just to focus on one difficulty, RT isn't thrown by multiple problems. For example, for the child with a genetic disability, living in a poor neighbourhood, and feeling depressed, it can be overwhelming knowing where to begin. RT offers a way to unravel the challenges by thinking about the five potions as a whole and making choices about what to work on with the child. It also brings the research together in one pot, and makes it accessible to parents and workers.

Parent: His problem is neurological, nothing can fix that.

RT Parent: Sounds like you already know from hard experience that there is no quick fix. And sometimes we have to face up to the painful fact that we can't repair certain things. But RT shows that even little things can help, and it gives you ways of making small changes. And in your case, perhaps it is particularly important to focus on getting as many positive vibes as possible from things that seem very small.

Parent: I am desperate to know what to do. They just want to delve into my family past and keep suggesting things I should do differently at home. It's okay for them, they don't have to live with him 24/7, shouting and screaming, punching his sister, breaking things. It's me who needs to be resilient.

RT Parent: Put your head in a bucket and scream very loudly. You're right, sounds like there is nothing to be done and we cannot help – but why not take a little peek at the next chapters anyway, just in case!

Sometimes it can all seem so serious, so we've tried to provide a few laughs along the way because while it might seem a bit cheeky, it's surprising how a touch of humour can get us through most situations.

The parents we've tried RT with so far have provided very encouraging feedback.

> The by-product of learning about resilience is that I have been bolstered myself.
>
> It's changed my lens and made me notice things I didn't notice before.
>
> It's an attitude shift. We spend so much time focusing on what our kids can't do that it can end up being a very sore place to be. We're so aware of where they're not hitting the mark or crisis managing that we can forget to look for the positives.

Some really appreciated having a pick and mix toolkit and said they liked being able to make choices about what they tried with their children. Others said it had helped them rethink things they were doing and experiment with new ways of managing difficulties at home. They also said it had helped them confront the trickier areas they would rather pretend weren't happening. They commented on how RT had encouraged them to notice their children's strengths and talents for managing hurdles and they said they felt better for it.

> I asked him how he felt when he went to school and he said he didn't want to go because they'd take the mickey out of him. But the really interesting thing for me was thinking actually he coped really really well with it and I was very pleasantly surprised. He has a brilliant sense of humour and so we rehearsed things he could do. RT has encouraged me to look at situations from both his and my own point of view, and now I draw on both to try to problem solve different scenarios and giggle too.

If you fancy rethinking some of your routines, want some new tips to help build your child's self-esteem and confidence or are looking for extra ideas to assist your child to roll with the knocks and punches of life then read on…RT can help.

Starting out: Becoming a resilient therapist

Where do I begin?

The main tool each of us brings to raising children is ourselves. But becoming a resilient therapist means combining this understanding with actively viewing yourself as your child's helper or therapist.

This may sound odd and we suspect it might even feel quite alien at first, as it's not the usual way of thinking about parenting. But deciding to become your child's resilient therapist requires a very deliberate decision on your part. It's about consciously helping children to find better ways to manage life's difficulties.

When we use the term 'therapist' we don't mean the detached and aloof figure who treats and analyses from a distance behind the patient's couch. Instead, we have in mind something a bit more 'hands on' like massage, yoga, art and play therapy or even retail therapy too. We mean something much more applied, with a focus on doing. It's about helping children to bring about some kind of change that makes their lives more fulfilling and enjoyable. So for example, helping them to change the way they think, feel or talk or maybe helping them to change their actions or behaviours. It's not all about big changes either; sometimes it can mean helping them to stay constant so that things don't get worse.

What we're suggesting is that you draw on all that you bring to your parenting, like your love, understanding and intuitive knowledge of your child, and add to this the idea of being strategic when you're making decisions about how to assist them to manage life more resiliently. Of course, you will be doing this already, but we hope this book will give you a few more tips.

So how do you become a child's resilient therapist? We think it's wise to start with two things: reflect on your own resilient approach and sign up to the RT noble truths to help get into a resilient way of thinking. This chapter explains these first steps and sets you up for the journey to learn more about using RT in your daily life and work.

Reflecting on your own resilient approach

Let's face it, raising children with complex needs can be tough. But applying some of the ideas of RT to yourself can not only strengthen your own capacity to bounce back if necessary, but can also help you to get a feel for what's needed to promote your children's ability to do the same. As one parent said:

> You can't teach a child to read if you haven't learnt to read yourself.

Parents and workers already using RT say it helps them to feel more able to beat the odds themselves.

> I thought learning about RT was going to be all about him and it hasn't at all been all about him. It's been about my attitude to him

and my attitude to myself as well. It's given me much more of an insight into me. It's built my resilience too.

It makes sense to acknowledge and understand your thoughts and feelings as best you can and take some time to get familiar with your own resilient ways, before expecting to be able to show children how to do the same. To help children come at life in resilient ways, you need to understand what resilient resources you've drawn on in your own life and how to build more.

So let's start with a memory exercise. What do you have in your resilience resource bank that makes you the parent you are? Before you do this exercise, here are some examples from other parents:

> I grew up in a really poor neighbourhood, but I was lucky enough to be brainy and applied myself so I did well in school. Education is still really important to me and I always help my children with their homework.

> When I was at school I found study difficult and didn't see the point of it. But I was lucky to have an economics teacher who made the lessons fun as well as challenging. It made me believe I could do something academic and so I help my kids see that learning can be enjoyable.

> I had a neighbour who used to watch our puppet shows. Her encouragement helped me to be more creative and gave me the confidence to perform. This taught me that it's good to support my children in their creativity.

> I had quite severe dyslexia but my mum encouraged me to look after my friend's dog and that got me a good job in a pet shop. I passed on my love of animals to my children.

> My brother was being bullied at school and, after talking to my dad, he decided that the only way to stop it was to confront the ring-leader and it worked. So now he's more willing to take the initiative. It makes him check that his daughter isn't being bullied and he encourages her to be proactive.

Don't worry if you weren't in the mood to do this right now, or if it didn't make much sense. Some parents have told us that they found this exercise difficult, others said it was quite easy, but whichever applies, it's useful to notice the possible link between what happened to you as a child and your parenting role now. So notice, was it easy to come up with

YOUR RESILIENCE RESOURCE BANK

1. Think back to your own childhood. Can you remember *anything* that helped you to bounce back or do better than you might have thought you would?

2. *Or*, if you can't think of anything, think of someone you know. What's helped them to be resilient in their childhood?

lots of examples? If it wasn't, is there someone you could ask to help you think about this or, even better, someone who knew you as a child to help you reflect on it? Getting in touch with what helped you as a child can help to think about what might help your own children. Standing back in this way can also help you consider your own parenting style and whether it's as positive as you want it to be.

All children have the potential to manage their lives resiliently. By learning the language and skills of RT we can encourage resilient ways of managing hard times – through the things we say, what we do and the opportunities and care we offer. And if we demonstrate resilient ways of managing our own lives children can begin to learn how to become more resilient themselves.

So with your own children in mind, have a go at charting how resiliently you think they're managing life's challenges at the moment. A quick reminder of what we mean by resilience: things that happen or resources we put in place that improve the odds for a child where they are stacked against them.

Knowing where you and your children are on the scale can help you make some decisions about where to put your efforts. Don't worry if you're off the scale completely! Be aware that it's just a snapshot in time. Where you mark the scale is likely to fluctuate all the time. Even in one day, you could chart your situation differently in the morning, afternoon and again in the evening. And as we said earlier, resilience is not 'in' a child so this is not about assessing whether they are to be unhelpfully labelled as resilient or unresilient.

It's not where you are on the scale that matters so much as having a visual way of thinking about your situation so you can reflect on your own starting point. Parents who tried this exercise found it quite revealing and they even suggested other parents might like to date the line and

---

WALK THE RESILIENT LINE

Even though we've written this book for parents of children with complex needs, you can use RT for all children. We've given you space for three children, but you can copy out more lines if needed.

Mark an x on this line from 1–10 to show how resiliently you think your child is managing life's challenges at the moment.

Not very resiliently   Very resiliently

0 10

Not very resiliently   Very resiliently

0 10

Not very resiliently   Very resiliently

0 10

Now chart how resilient you feel in relation to each child. You could use a different coloured pen, or initial a separate mark to chart yourself in relation to them.˙

---

do it again in a few months' time after they've tried using some of the RT potions and strategies.

> I've actually realized it's my daughter who isn't special needs and is very bright and doing very well, but is so insecure it's amazing. She's the one I'm using all the strategies for and, if I hadn't done this line, it wouldn't have occurred to me. It would have gone straight over my head, thinking she was fine. It was a real eye opener for me.

> That line we did was quite a revelation for me. I wanted to learn about RT for my middle son because he has ADHD and Asperger's but I actually thought he is incredibly resilient and it was my resilience in relation to him and dealing with him that was the factor.

> My resilience with my son is low but his is high, whereas my resilience with my daughter is high and hers is low. So whether your

score and your child's are similar or very different, it helped me see it clearly and increased my awareness about it.

Getting into a resilient way of thinking

Learning to routinely think resiliently is an important step towards becoming a resilient therapist. So far, we've asked you to get a feel for where you and your child are at when it comes to thinking and acting resiliently. Getting to grips with the four noble truths is our next port of call. This should give you some more tools to help you.

We've used the idea of noble truths as a way of thinking about the basis or the underlying beliefs or values that we consider important to making RT work for children and their families. This doesn't mean they're easy to achieve and we know everybody acts against their better judgement at times, but they are principles to strive for and return to when things get overwhelming.

The *four noble truths* of RT are:

- **Acceptance** – starting with exactly where your child is at even if it means being at a very sore point.

- **Conservation** – holding onto any good that has happened up until now and building on it.

- **Commitment** – staying in there but being realistic about what's doable and not giving up or expecting things to change overnight.

- **Enlisting** – asking for help from the right people and moving on from those who might have let you down in the past.

We thought these seemed straightforward enough and easy to understand, but we soon found them a bit more demanding to apply. In our experience they challenge each and every one of us on a daily basis. Let's have a look at them more closely.

THE NOBLE TRUTH OF ACCEPTING

This is probably one of the most important things you have to do to be a resilient therapist. It's the backbone of your resilient practice. And we think it's the hardest. Why? Because we both reckon parenting is the most demanding job we have ever had. Would you apply for this job?

WANTED – PARENTS TO RAISE CHILDREN WITH COMPLEX NEEDS

Dedicated adults needed to work in a busy, demanding and fraught working environment. This is a long-term position so you must have staying power, excellent communication skills and the ability to plan and organize family life for everyone. No previous experience required but you will need to be a good negotiator, determined to make the most of things, and have an excellent sense of humour.

Main purpose of the job
To raise happy children by taking the lead for their day to day care.

Tasks involved

* To be flexible and adjust swiftly to bad news even if crumbling inside.

* To expose your life to professionals and ask for help from others.

* To understand child development without basic training or information.

* To anticipate children's needs at every stage of their life.

* To teach children new skills regardless of their age, ability or impairment.

* To identify problems and assess situations even when unsure yourself.

* To keep things ticking over, pay the bills, manage the budget and share it out fairly.

* To learn on the job and promote clever solutions at a moment's notice.

* To negotiate disputes even when all are behaving badly.

* To keep track of records and reports when you'd rather forget the bad news.

* To control yourself when it feels like it's all too hard to manage and you want to explode.

* To be consistently kind and look like you're enjoying it all the time.

* To keep your spirits up even when you're feeling tired, unsupported or criticized.

* To stay in there through thick and thin and be grown up and responsible even when you are bored, exasperated and want to behave like a teenager.

Pay: Not much. You're doing this for love.

There is no way anyone would be queuing for an application for this post of perfect parent. The job is not doable, the expectations are unreasonable and the qualities and tasks are unrealistic.

Message for professionals
Would you apply for this job? Which bits could you do?

What's amazing to us is how frequently we come across parents who think they should be able to do it all! And worse still, even when they are doing a brilliant job, they don't recognize it, or they stay focused on the things they don't do so well.

Parenting in a resilient way means accepting the reality – noticing the little things you do that make a difference and allowing yourself to simply be good enough.

There really isn't a world of perfect parents out there, just as there isn't a world of perfect children. Can you imagine a similar job description for the perfect child?

WANTED – CHILDREN TO MAKE FAMILY LIFE PERFECT

Smiling, undemanding and obedient children needed to fulfil the fantasy of a continually happy family life. You must be full of love, innocent, giving and kind hearted. Good manners would be a definite asset. You must be able to amuse and entertain yourself and move on to an independent adult life. You need to be predictable, willing to communicate your needs calmly and fit in happily with what others in the family want to do.

Parents are often very good at noticing and celebrating the good moments and the positive things about their children. Accepting ourselves and our children when we and they fall short of the ideal isn't always as easy. Acknowledging your children for who they are and what they've done can be really difficult when, for example, their behaviour has driven you to distraction.

> How many times can you put up with getting your house trashed, I wonder? I've tried everything. I've even locked him in the toilet hoping he'll calm down but he climbed out the window and the neighbours called the police. He's bigger than me, I can't control him, it's impossible. The medication's not working. He just kicks off when he gets in. Yesterday, he kicked the door down, he was in such a rage.

> I feel guilty saying it, but it gets so tedious when she goes on and on about how worried she is about everything. Other kids her age just walk down to the park on their own. It shouldn't be a big deal but the effort I have to put in to help her get down there for five minutes is astonishing.

> I try to be understanding, but if she comes down one more time at 11 p.m. to tell me she can't get to sleep because she's fretting about what the children at school think about her (half of whom seem to be kids she doesn't even know), I'll go mad.

It's hard being around children when they're off the wall, violent with anger, constantly withdrawn, miserable or unwilling to take responsibility for themselves. Knowing how best to help them to manage their lives more resiliently relies on knowing where they are at. So getting some distance and assessing their situations is key.

Parents often tell us how fed up they feel when professionals spend all their time assessing their children. This is usually because they feel they don't then get on and do anything. What we're suggesting here is that when we fully accept our children we take account of and accept their histories and their current situations, and we use this knowledge to guide our decisions about what to try next. It informs our actions. This is why it's so helpful when professionals actually read the files and are up to date. Making choices about what to do next are made on the strength of what we already know about children and what's worked and not worked in the past.

An RT approach accepts that life is messy and often unfair. For some children, disadvantage comes in many shapes and sizes and often all at once. Unfortunately, sad and bad things happen to really nice people all the time.

> It's like being hit with a mallet, isn't it?

> I was frantically making out that it was going to be alright, although I really knew that there was something wrong… I was fighting it all along.

> My older son is a square peg in a round hole, just like me. For the first nine years of his life I tried to push the square peg into the round hole. Now I am going, okay so where are the square holes and how do we get to the square holes?

How we relate to our situations, to our children and to the others around us can make a world of difference. Even though you may not be satisfied with your parenting all the time and your children may not be exactly the children you hoped for, it is what you have. And you will know that there's not much use having a 'permanent pout' because the world is not the way we want it to be. Finding ways to construct a life that is good despite the worries and disappointments is, in our opinion, worth the effort.

> Once I really accepted that she's not going to change dramatically, I was able to put more energy into the little things that might realistically help us rather than wishing she was more like my friends' kids.

We don't mean to underestimate the feelings of sadness, the adapting or all the hard work involved, which can leave parents and even professionals feeling glum. We know the difficulties can often take over and dominate our thinking and no wonder when you glance at some of the research findings that clearly show how the odds are stacked against children with disabilities and special educational needs.

We weren't sure about including the next box because we were worried it was too negative. But we decided we should leave it in because it really brings it home that this is the sort of territory parents and children are managing every day. Being reminded of and acknowledging these inequalities helps explain why we can get so fed up sometimes and need help to fight the feelings of doom and gloom. And it might even remind you that you are not alone.

Accepting doesn't mean there aren't things that we want to change, nor fears or injustices so strongly felt that we're driven to search for solutions. Some things are just too hard to manage and responsibility for what is happening ought to be borne collectively and rests with society. We know some things are almost unbearable but we think this probably makes it even more important to make a few active decisions about where to concentrate your efforts. One parent pointed us to the Serenity

DID YOU KNOW...

- Children with special educational needs are 13 times more likely to be excluded from school than other children.

- One in ten children suffer from mental illness severe enough to affect their functioning. (Fonagy et al. 2002).

- Parent carers are less likely to have support networks or informal childcare arrangements with friends and neighbours.

- Parents of children with special needs are vulnerable to high levels of stress, leading to disproportionate levels of depression, chronic fatigue and negative feelings about being a parent.

- Caring for a disabled child can cause relationship problems. One study reveals that 31% of couples say they have some problems, 13% cite major problems and 9% actually separate. (For statistics on disability see the Contact a Family (CAF) details in Resources at the end of the book.)

Prayer which she thought summed it up beautifully, which goes something like 'grant me the serenity to accept the things I cannot change, courage to change the things I can, and the wisdom to know the difference' (see McAfee Brown 1987, p.251).

> I found it challenging and emotionally painful. What I get from RT is actually nothing is insurmountable, wherever you start from is fine, and you can build on what you already have.

RT can help us stay creative and objective in response to the daily challenges of raising children with complex needs.

THE NOBLE TRUTH OF CONSERVING

Stepping outside of your life and looking in is a really helpful way of combating the doom and gloom attitude we can all get stuck in. We call this becoming your own observer. It's a great way to 'conserve' or hang onto and look after the things that seem to work well.

This might appear obvious but we've found over time that there's a whole load of information about our children and what's gone well with them in the past that we forget to draw on when we're in the thick of it. And the reverse can also be true. Maybe there was something you tried when they were younger that didn't work so you don't use it any more. Now that they're a little older, it might in fact be worth giving another go.

Conserving is like going on an archaeological dig. You're trying to carefully unearth little signs of worthwhile things from the past. Often building a child's resilience is about building on the strengths they already have. The challenge can be digging these up and calling them to mind when you really need them. Assuming a degree of detachment and getting a bit of distance can help. Here's an exercise to help you get hold of a slightly different angle on a situation.

Imagine you were outdoors, peering through the window of your home, watching your family life. What do you see on a good day?

WHAT DO YOU SEE?

When do things at home with your children work best? When are things a bit more settled or happy? List the times or occasions here.

Now, pinpoint what it is about these times that make things a little easier. What are some of the ingredients?

Getting used to being your own observer takes a bit of practice and time but what you're looking for are examples and incidents from the past that you can call to mind to use in new situations. It's about transplanting the good from one circumstance to another, even if this means only pulling out one tiny aspect from that past experience.

Sometimes we can forget what we've got to work with when it's right under our noses but finding a way to first pinpoint your children's strengths, however small, and hooking into these is a really useful thing to do.

Try this on yourself.

UNEARTHING LITTLE GEMS

Imagine…someone who knows you well is describing you.

What would they say were your helpful characteristics?

Now, think of a situation with your child that you find too hard to manage.

Which of these characteristics can you call on and use in these situations?

Now, imagine answering the same questions with your child in mind. What are their helpful characteristics that can be called upon to use in difficult situations?

We're going on about this because we know how hard it is to remember those little things, even though doing so can help avoid getting stuck into a negative downward spiral.

Building simple routines into your daily schedule that help you capture and hang onto the good bits can mean the difference between having a good or a bad day. And frankly, we're very interested in increasing the number of good days. Here are a few examples of things parents have told us they do to conserve those little things.

Tips from parents

- Put positive post-it notes on the mobile phone.

- Record the little successes in a Family Golden Book – you can take it out and read it when times are particularly tough.

- Look at photos and video clips of good times.

- Get back in touch with good people you've lost contact with from the past.

- Read over your children's school reports searching for positive comments and for ideas of things you can encourage in them.

- Have things they've done (e.g. pictures) past and present up next to each other on the wall to show how they've moved on.

- Revisit positive experiences verbally, e.g. 'Do you remember when you...?'

- Revisit bad times so you can acknowledge how things have moved.

- Briefly remind yourself of the most hideous time you've ever had, and notice how it's still not as bad now.

We don't mean to underestimate the task involved in learning to manage the complexity of your situations. In our experience, sometimes it's just about appreciating the little things that make the tiniest of difference that get parents through and keep us thinking resiliently.

> I think I was looking for more and I didn't realize it was as simple. I see RT as a very simple idea for very complicated people. I feel I have very complicated issues...but if I do practise the RT ideas, it works. I've got a very immediate positive response from both my children.

> He's in a school that's right for him at last. It was hard getting him in. It's so important to remember what we have achieved so far and not forget it.

> RT reminds you of times that were better, and the fact that I do feel quite resilient most of the time – I think to myself, it's here some-where, I just need to dig for it.

THE NOBLE TRUTH OF COMMITMENT

Parenting children with complex needs is often a job for life and you know you are in for the long haul. So getting your head around what making a commitment involves rarely causes parents any confusion.

Most get on with it, even though the hours are terrible, there's no pension, support is thin on the ground and it's not something you can change your minds about very easily, if at all.

But what if, deep down, you'd rather not be doing it? What if you wish you'd never become a parent of a child with complex needs? How do we manage those conflicting feelings?

It's possible that the first thing you might need to do is to acknowledge these feelings for yourself. We reckon it can take a lot more energy and effort to pretend we don't have certain thoughts and feelings as it does to admit them to ourselves! This doesn't mean you're a bad parent, it simply means you're human and it's probably a signal, from you to you, that you could do with some extra support. RT can help you get to the point where you might actually get some.

But it's likely that there will always be times when it's just down to you. Unlike professionals, who can choose their area of work and go home at the end of the day and try to switch off, it can be really hard for parents to come to terms with the absence of choice and the ongoing nature of the job. Your days are long and it's not so easy to move onto something else even though you're feeling worn out!

DID YOU KNOW...

98% of disabled children live at home with their family of origin into adult years. (See the CAF factsheet; details are in Resources at the end of this book.)

We think it's important not to assume or take for granted continual parental commitment. And it helps not to assume that professionals aren't struggling sometimes too. What if your job is not what you thought it would be? What if you feel as though little you do has any effect, or even worse, that there is not much that can be done anyway? What if you're bored and fed up? How do you become a resilient therapist when you're managing feelings like this? Here we suggest some strategies to keep the commitment going.

Maybe meeting up with people who are managing similar situations would help. Parents frequently tell us how useful it is to meet parents in the 'same boat' because, in sharing the worst and the best together, they say they feel less isolated. And they say the best tips and the best medicine comes from other parents. And keeping a sense of hope is one of the positive things professionals tell us they get from peer support and peer supervision.

We laughed about the most awful things.

Another idea is that it helps to have a strategy at hand, ready to call on at a moment's notice to help you get things back into perspective. One way to do this is to link the state of mind you want, such as those pleasant feelings about being a parent or a family support worker, to a chosen touch, word or something visual to help you recollect these nice feelings and call them to mind easily. It's called 'anchoring' and goes like this. Imagine you get nervous about doing exams and you freeze. Anchoring suggests that you instead focus on what it feels like to manage the exams well, and to link this positive feeling with a consciously chosen stimulus, like stroking your arm, or using a specific word, for example. Then if you practise linking this feeling with the stimulus, you can train yourself to easily access that feeling at will, whenever you need it, particularly when you have an exam. It's like teaching your body and your mind to recognize certain stimuli as triggers for desired states of mind.

So, find such a stimulus to help you call to mind those good feelings when you notice them slipping away, and practise it. Get it lodged into your memory ready to call on when you feel yourself getting glum.

We asked a small of group of parents if they had found any easy ways to manage those awful days and here are a few ideas from them:

Tips from parents

- Breathe consciously and deliberately; take really big breaths.

- Notice the good things, call them to mind, visualize them clearly.

- Contact that person who can remind you you're doing a good job.

- Exercise or get a massage to ease the tension out of your body.

- Learn to release your anger, practise ways to get it out like punching pillows, hard exercise, shouting loudly.

- Find ways and things that guarantee you a good laugh.

- Get in touch with someone you can be irreverent with and won't judge you.

- Find out about options for the future. Know the career, college or residential placement options for your child.

- Keep a sense of humour. Look back at those times that were awful, but now seem funny.

- Remember that tomorrow is another day and this time will pass.

- Just one more hour.

Some of you may be shocked at us suggesting there could be times when you wish you didn't have your children and you might be thinking, 'I've never wished this ever.' Others might have only just realized you've been wishing this all your life but were too embarrassed to admit it to yourself, let alone anyone else. The point is, whatever it is you feel is fine, because the fact is, irrespective of these darker moments, you're staying in there even when there may be times when you wish you weren't.

According to the resilience research and the studies on programmes aimed at supporting children managing significant disadvantage, staying in there is hugely important. Recognize it, and give yourself a proper pat on the back for being so committed. And we know from what parents have told us that having a committed and consistent worker can also make a world of difference.

When we've talked with professionals about commitment, they were worried about encouraging dependency. They talked of the constraints of time, the dangers of becoming too close and an awareness of their own limits and capacity for emotional commitment when they were seeing so many children and families with unmet need. And when we talked with parents about commitment, they spoke of being over-involved and struggling to get a distance from their child's problems.

You feel it for them.

I'm so worn out I think I've just switched off from it all. I'm almost done caring.

Thinking about commitment as a basis for becoming a resilient therapist appears a little more complex than we had first imagined. While we know there's a whole debate about professional boundaries, we also know that finding ways to establish good trusting relationships and offering reliable and predictable contact is crucial to making a difference to the lives of disadvantaged children. There are no quick fixes for children and families managing the level of disadvantage we mentioned in the 'Did you know…' box. And we don't know of any studies that show short-term inputs produce long-term good outcomes for this group of children.

However, making a commitment to be there for the long haul doesn't mean you have to forget your own needs. Getting the right balance between being over or under-involved is a skill worth learning.

Setting low expectations or doing the minimum can sometimes be an understandable but unhelpful way of protecting ourselves from the fear of failure. The scale of the task and our own self-doubt can get in the way of remembering the expertise, objectivity and skill we can offer a situation.

Children can be completely overwhelmed by their feelings, and you can too. If you're not careful, before you know it, our kids' emotions can land in our laps and we find ourselves feeling almost the same. You have to get some distance. It's a bit like helping children when they're being bullied at school. Listening to them tell you that they are being bullied is distressing. It can flood back old memories of being pushed around ourselves, and make us feel angry and hugely protective. But what helps is, if we can stay calm, showing that we can cope with what they have told us. Getting a bit of distance and enough perspective on the situation positions us in a stronger place to be useful to them.

And if you are a professional reading this, we understand that talking about commitment can make some feel anxious and overwhelmed, and you may have very strong views about it. Knowing where your boundaries are and communicating that certainly helps. And you don't necessarily have to see children and their families every week to communicate your commitment. Reflecting on what time you can offer, whether in person, on the phone, via email or indirectly, is worth the effort. Then you'll know if you're overloaded with work, or simply can't face putting the effort into a particular family. And be honest and open about how long you're staying around. If you know you're leaving your job in two months' time, make sure everyone knows that. Using some basic psychoanalytic principles helps too. By this we mean giving people precise times when they will see you, and sticking to that. And letting them know when and where you are available to be contacted.

THE NOBLE TRUTH OF ENLISTING

Remember the parent job description we mentioned earlier? We're convinced that you cannot raise children with complex needs alone. The job needs more than one person to pull it off successfully! Enlisting is about sharing out the tasks – your task as a resilient therapist is to get others involved.

But how do you do this, when there doesn't seem to be too many willing to stick around for long? Or when it can take an age to get the right people together for a simple discussion? How do you get others involved when you have little experience of asking for help?

Most of us have different people in our lives for different reasons. Some people we tell some things to, other people we tell other things to. We share different activities with different people and so on. People serve different purposes in our lives. So you have to get strategic about finding the right people to bring on board. But you need to be careful to strike a balance between having too many versus not enough. The last thing you want to do is to undermine your efforts to strengthen your child because too many people are involved and confusing things further. And unless you're in the right space for it, you don't want to create another job for yourself co-ordinating everyone else, unless of course you've agreed to take this keyworker role on.

More often than not, parents have plenty of experience expecting family, friends or services to be involved, only to find that many disappear along the way.

Taking responsibility to recruit the help of others isn't always easy, particularly if your child has just been excluded from school again for difficult behaviour or their self-esteem is so low they're anything but a bundle of laughs to be around. So put yourself in others' shoes. Why might they want to be enlisted? What might they get out of it? Here are some ideas:

What's in it for others to get involved with your child?

- A chance to feel good about helping you out.

- Money or some other practical reward.

- Career experience.

- A chance to practise new skills.

- The opportunity to spend time with my funny, interesting child.

- An insight into the world of children with special needs.

- A chance to do childlike things that are hard to do without a child.

- The opportunity to slow down a bit and do simple things.

- The chance to feel important and needed.

With this in mind, you might like to have a go at the 'Talent Spotting' exercise on the next page to help you enlist the right talent.

I keep a look out for people I can 'friend up'.

It can be really healthy and beneficial to develop communities of people around you who appreciate and value the effort you and your child are making. Find ways to call their presence to mind when things are tough.

> I had this awful meeting. I knew they were going to skirt about things and not talk about the real issues. I was quite scared because I clam up at those things. But I remembered my friend and how she really believes my son deserves a proper education like any other child, so I imagined what she would say. It helped me to speak up... She'd be proud of me.

You don't need us to remind you that it can make a world of difference when professionals ally with parents who are running out of steam. Remember, it can be helpful to find people with authority, professional status and expert knowledge to help you and even act on your behalf sometimes.

By now, you should have a good idea of what we mean by the noble truths and how we can put each of them – accepting, conserving, commitment and enlisting – into practice. Our final job in this chapter is to introduce the Magic Box of potions and remedies. These are designed to help us apply the ideas of resilience research to real life.

The Magic Box

We mentioned earlier that we had found it helpful to think about RT visually. We suggested a Magic Box of five different potions and

TALENT SPOTTING – FINDING PEOPLE WITH THE TALENTS YOU NEED

Who do you know (other than yourself), in your life who has the following talents?

- Good at finding out what's going on and knows about fun things to do with children.

  ....

- Is prepared to go to the park even though my child runs off often or won't take turns on the swings.

  ....

- Cooks and is relaxed about preparing large family meals. ....

- Practical and good at getting their hands dirty.

  ....

- Is a good listener and hard to shock.

  ....

- Can handle conflict, doesn't mind disagreements and can be your advocate. ....

- Understands the way big organizations work.

  ....

- Someone willing to go out with you to have fun.

  ....

These are just a few examples – add your own things to the list that others might be able to do, that you would find really supportive.

remedies from which you can choose what's needed to strengthen a child. But it may be that the idea of 'magic' seems a bit frivolous or unscientific to some.

Really there's no magic you know, it's just about keeping at it.

Continually searching for ways to support children to make their lives work in more resilient ways is definitely the task of a resilient therapist.

Being determined and unshakable in that search are fantastic assets. We have deliberately used the word 'magic' because we think being a resilient therapist involves a touch of concocting a creative mix, with a dash of art, a splash of science and a touch of measuring quantities and combinations. While we know from the research on resilience that there are potions that are useful in almost all situations, RT is also a bit magical because the when, how or why a certain combination of factors has a good effect can surprise us.

Finding the right potion holds an element of trial and error, mixing and matching and conjuring up new solutions. It's about listening, acting on informed hunches and interweaving all this to give things a go, because you believe you can make a difference.

> It's about maybe dealing with one potion at a time, finding what the best fit is at that particular space in time and dealing with that, so it's much more manageable.

There's also an element of the unknown at play here. The resilience research doesn't yet tell us what will work best for each situation or individual child, nor does it tell us what to try first or what to prioritize. But it does mention, time and time again, those significant moments in life that lead us to follow one path over another, that works out for the better. If you were to reflect on such a moment in your own life, could you pinpoint what it was that caused you to take that better path, at that particular moment in time? We suspect that sometimes it's clear and sometimes it's not so obvious at all. And so it is with RT.

However, if you don't like the idea of a Magic Box, don't let the language put you off. Think of RT as a pick and mix toolkit instead, and skip over any irritating references to 'magic' wherever you can! Think of the potions and remedies as a treasure chest of ideas from which you can pick and choose what to try. Use the language that suits you best.

The five RT potions

What's in the toolkit? So what are these five potions from which you can conjure ways to build your child's ability to respond to life resiliently? There's an illustration of the Magic Box and a table at the end of this chapter. In a nutshell, the five RT potions are:

- Basics

- Belonging

- Learning
- Coping
- Core Self.

Basics is about getting the necessities needed for life sorted. Helping your children to get a good night's sleep, putting a decent meal on the table and keeping them warm in the winter are the sort of things that we can forget to acknowledge as huge everyday achievements. This potion reminds us to remember the significance of these basic things, like checking your housing is okay, that you have enough money to live, that you feel safe, have the means to get out and about, enjoy a healthy diet, get some exercise and fresh air and have the chance to have fun.

Belonging puts good relationships at the heart of things. It focuses on reminding us to have and look after healthy relationships and to tap into good influences instead of bad ones. It recommends concentrating on the good times and places, find people our children can count on and remain hopeful about building new contacts.

Learning reminds us to look after our children's learning. This doesn't just mean sorting their schooling, although this is really important, it's also about the less formal ways they learn. Like making sure they develop interests, talents and life skills. And daring to have a vision for a life plan or a future full of doing new things. It reminds us to help children to get organized, notice their achievements and develop new skills. And it all goes for us parents too, encouraging us to do things like follow up new and old interests for ourselves.

Coping is about those things we and our children can do to help us get by in everyday life. Like those times when they need to be brave, solve problems and stand up for their own views and beliefs. It's about putting on rose-tinted glasses if necessary, looking after their talents, learning the art of staying calm, remembering that tomorrow's a new day and leaning on others when necessary. Not hard to see how this one might be of particular interest to us as well!

Core Self focuses on children's inner worlds. It's about those thoughts and beliefs they have about themselves that build their characters. This potion concentrates on ways of being hopeful, guiding them to find their own sense of morality, drawing on all their senses (seeing, hearing, touching, tasting) to get a good solid sense of who they are. It encourages us to help children learn to take responsibility for themselves, face problems and seek help and treatment when it makes sense to do so.

Conclusion

Each of the chapters in the rest of this book will give you specific examples of what these potions mean in practice. You can use them individually or draw on the entire range, because we know that using any of the five potions has an effect on all of the others. Like ripples in a pond, they spread out and radiate from each other. While you might decide to use just a few of the ideas, the larger the pool of possibilities the more ripples and choice you have and the more flexible you can be in deciding how to use them in real-life situations.

> You go looking for strategies and different ways to deal with things and, what RT does, it gives you almost a checklist that you can tick and you say 'I *am* dealing with this', so you can tick them off and say, 'I do have this, I do do that, this is okay and that's okay.' It's almost like you can celebrate the things that you *are* doing and then it feels kind of like you have a lot less to deal with – like a shopping list – you start out at the supermarket, you've got 101 things that you have to go and find and, as you go round and tick them off, by the time you get to aisle 24, it's like done. But as you go through, there's less on the list to deal with so it feels manageable.

> I found I ended up analysing things in a slightly different manner. I mean you go through life as a parent of special needs kids, you're picking up strategies from wherever you can get them, be it parenting courses, other parents, professionals, whatever. RT comes at it from a slightly different angle – it's a whole new toolkit and you get a different slant on things. It offers ideas for how to cope and you don't have to be perfect all the time.

We hope we've managed to convince you of four things in this chapter:

1. Wherever you start from is okay.

2. It helps to reflect on your own resilient approach.

3. The four noble truths are an important place to begin.

4. Building a child's resilience will build your own.

I found the noble truths were fundamental. Not just for RT but also for keeping my own and my sons' lives on track.

RT is very immediate, very pick-upable. It's very easy to go, okay I will use that tool now…it's 'let's try it and see what happens'.

So in the rest of the book let's now introduce you to the five potions in more detail.

Table 1: Summary of child developmental stages

Approximate age range	Physical development	Intellectual development	Emotional development	Social development	Moral development
Baby BEING & DOING	Feeding a priority Sucking and grasping Reaches for things Large movements with arms and legs, rolls over Supports head Responds to voice, tone No bladder or bowel control	Makes sounds, babbles and chuckles Learns they have an impact on others	Attaches and bonds Develops feelings – cries, smiles, sucks thumb Focused on getting basic needs met, learns to trust it will happen	Recognizes carers Reliant on carers to get needs met so smiles and makes social contact	No sense of right or wrong Consider themselves the centre of the world
1–3 years Toddlers THINKING	Feeds self with spoon Crawls, stands, walks Can pick up small objects Can use finger and thumb to hold crayon Can draw a circle Has control of bladder and bowels	Starts to use words to name things Speech becomes clearer Fascinated by everything Looks for things that are out of sight Can draw a simple person shape, match and sort	Shows feelings and sympathy Can separate from main carers, uses 'I' and 'me' Recognizes people outside of the home Imitates adult behaviour	World expands and bonds with others outside the home Tests boundaries Says 'no' Gets frustrated when can't do things co-operatively	Beginning to learn right from wrong Understands self in relation to others

Approximate age range	Physical development	Intellectual development	Emotional development	Social development	Moral development
3–6 years Preschoolers INDEPENDENCE	Better control and balance for hopping, skipping and dancing Draws faces with detail Improved fine motor skills Can write simple letters and draw a neat square	Uses sentences Makes up stories Has likes and dislikes Asks questions Can do puzzles Can draw a whole person	Identifies happy and sad feelings in others Imitates carers Can tolerate being further away from carers Often overwhelmed by feelings	Dresses and undresses Make believe play Follows simple rules Starts to share, take turns Begins to show manners Wants more independence Tests authority, shows off	Protects themself Stands up for their rights Notices what behaviour brings rewards Needs external controls as conscience not formed
6–12 years School age SKILLS	Energetic Plays sports, rides a bike Growing fast, big appetite Well-developed fine motor skills Writing and drawing with ease	Very verbal, tells jokes Curious – often asks why, when, how questions Notices reading, writing, maths are important and wants to do well Likes task-focused activity Understands past, present, future	Sure of themselves but also silly sometimes Likes affection and wants carers to be around Can identify their feelings Understands difference between desires, motives and actions	Joins in local activities Enjoys being with others Has friends but can be alone too Plays mostly with same sex peers Learns to achieve and compete	Begins to notice conflict between views of adults and peers Rules are important and should be followed Strong sense of fairness Able to make conscious decisions

We constructed this table by looking at a number of different versions of child development stages which included: Erikson's 8 Stages of Psychosocial Development (Cole and Cole 1989); Piaget's Stages of Cognitive Development (Mussen 1983; and Kohlberg's Theory of Moral Reasoning (Kohlberg 1984) – but remember, it's just a summary.

Basics - this potion conjures up the basic necessities needed for life

Belonging - this potion is about ways to help a child make good relationships with family and friends

Coping - the remedies in this potion help children get by in everyday life

Learning - includes school education as well as ways of helping with their life skills, talents and interests

Core self - the spells here work very deeply to help shape a child's character

BOX

accepting conserving
commitment enlisting

M
A
G
I
C

RESILIENT THERAPY: ORDINARY MAGIC

Angie Hart &/Derek Blincow©

Table 2: Resilient Therapy summary

	Nobel truths: Accepting; Conserving; Commitment; Enlisting			
Basics	**Belonging**	**Learning**	**Coping**	**Core Self**
Enough money to live	Find somewhere for the child to belong	Make school life work as well as possible	Understand boundaries and keep to them	Instil a sense of hope
Good enough housing	Help child understand his/her place in the world	Engage mentors for children	Be brave	Help the child to know him/herself
Being safe	Tap into good influences	Map out career or life plan	Solve problems	Teach the child to understand other people's feelings
Play and leisure opportunities	Keep relationships going	Develop life skills	Put on rose-tinted glasses	Help the child take responsibility for her/himself
Exercise and fresh air	The more healthy relationships the better	Help the child to organize her/himself	Foster their interests	Foster their talents
Access to transport	Take what you can from any relationship where there is some hope	Highlight achievements	Calm her/himself down, self-soothe	There are tried and tested treatments for specific problems; use them
Healthy diet	Get together people the child can count on		Remember that tomorrow is another day	
	Responsibilities and obligations		Lean on others when necessary	
	Focus on good times and places			
	Make sense of where the child has come from			
	Predict a good experience of someone/something new			
	Make friends and mix with other children			

CHAPTER 1

BASICS

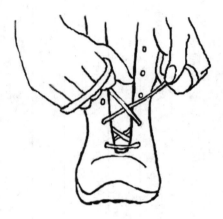

In the introduction we asked you to reflect on your approach; now we want to suggest some action.

Basics is the first of the five RT potions and we've put it right up front, because it's all about getting the necessities needed for life. Like having enough money, a shelter over our heads, feeling safe, being able to get out and about, eating and exercising reasonably well and getting a break when we need it.

And guess what, you might find this chapter boring but the fact of the matter is that it may be the most important one you'll read. When you get the basics right, things can change dramatically sometimes. And while having a child with complex needs can pull us into examining the basics in a way we might never have considered before, often those very small things can make a huge difference to how we and our children manage what life throws at us.

We think that it really is worth getting into this stuff because children need the basics to build their resilience and we need them too.

Research shows that being mega rich doesn't lead to happiness but there is a link between doing okay financially – that's having some of the basics sorted – and being content in life. This chapter gives you the chance to notice what you're doing already and what could do with a bit more attention.

> You know it was the practical stuff that made the difference. If you haven't got the bottom line sorted, you'll keep running in circles like a hamster in a wheel.

It's understandable that parents are so worn down that they can end up losing out on the basics. And if you're a professional reading this, it's also easy to think either that it's someone else's job to help families to get these practical things sorted, or we should just shrug our shoulders and accept that this is the context within which we are working. But how on earth can we expect families to manage demanding things like adapting to the news, learning about their child's difficulties, new behaviour techniques or family therapy, if we haven't helped them to get the practical stuff sorted too?

> I'm busy with a star chart and his behaviour but meanwhile I can't even get his clothes washed for school. The washing machine's packed up, I don't have the money to get it fixed, he wets the bed every night, the sheets are stinking and piling up. But I'm so busy chasing after him that I can't get a moment to ring a plumber.

What we're suggesting here is the need to really sharpen our focus on the basics, dull though this is. For starters, let's really notice how unfair the world can be to children with complex needs and their families.

And did you know that people living in poorer neighbourhoods live shorter lives on average? There's loads of evidence now that getting basics like decent housing, a decent standard of living and a non-polluted environment is more important for good health than anything that the health service can do for us. So all the more reason to sort out the practical issues because they have a big impact on wellbeing.

Becoming a resilient therapist might mean you have to develop an 'inequalities imagination' – that's if you haven't got one already. By this we mean having an awareness of the impact of unfairness on children and being able to see that there are much larger forces at play than just what individual kids, mums or dads do. Understanding how systems can fail children, and taking note of how they can become the victims of disablism, poverty and a whole range of other inequalities through no

---

DID YOU KNOW...

- Four in ten parents of disabled children report living in unsuitable housing. (Oldman and Beresford 2002)
- Only 8% get any services from their local services. (CAF factsheet, see Resources at end of book)
- Bringing up a disabled child costs on average three times more than non-disabled children. (Dobson and Middleton 1998)
- One in seven families with disabled children are living in debt and are four times more likely than other families to have debts in excess of £10,000. (Harrison and Wolley 2004)

---

fault of their own, can really help us avoid thinking that everything is just about changing our child or ourselves. An inequalities imagination can help us get stuck in with a realistic sense of the unfairness of what is happening.

And so, with our sleeves rolled up and our determination intact, Basics confronts head on what a practical matter it is being disadvantaged.

But it's no easy task addressing the practical stuff. As a group, disabled children and young people with complex needs don't have much of a voice when it comes to arguing their corner. If you've got the talent to notice small gains when trying to get big systems and large bureaucracies to be flexible and responsive to your individual situation or circumstance, all the better. Unfortunately, sometimes you have to do battle, to get things done.

> I made thirteen phone calls, wrote seven letters and six emails. I nearly went and stood outside their office with a sandwich board but the carpenter came round to make the door wider just in time!

Sorting the necessities for life can be so trying that we think you should definitely be giving yourself rewards along the way just for hanging in there.

> I do deals with myself. I agree to fill in another three pages of the form, before I treat myself to sitting out in the garden for a while. As

it goes on, the time I spend working gets less and the time having breaks gets longer, but we start out well.

I imagine what my best friend would say if she was here: it's usually laugh, sit, a cup of tea, in that order.

Any ideas you have for relieving the boredom and relentless tedium of it all should be applied at every opportunity. If you're lucky enough to find a way to approach the task differently so that you get a sense of achievement from being on top of it all, then hang onto it. You could make a fortune bottling and selling it.

DID YOU KNOW...

We spend an average of 142 minutes a day doing housework. And if you're a woman, it rises to an average of 178 minutes a day. (Office of National Statistics 2005)

Having your own private secretary to sort filling in the next form or arrange the next hospital appointment might be a lovely dream but, sadly, it won't get the task done. You've got to find what works for you.

I can't be bothered to do any ironing, and prefer to spend the time relaxing in the bath getting used to my bad feelings about my kids going around in crumpled clothes.

With so many of us there's always a fight for the TV but the minute I put the ironing board up I'm trumping everybody. I'm ironing, I have to watch the TV.

Maybe one of the best places to start is to get the Basics sorted for yourself. Managing the everyday challenges well if we're stuck at home all the time, constantly worried about paying the bills or resorting to only eating comfort food, is unlikely to work. It can make a world of difference to feeling able to manage, if we look after our own Basics alongside looking after our children's.

Have a go at answering the following questions:

PARENT SELF-ASSESSMENT CHART

Parent self-assessment	True	False	Sometimes
1 I have enough money to have a decent enough standard of living.	☐	☐	☐
2 Our home is adequate to meet our needs.	☐	☐	☐
3 I feel safe and free from danger most of the time.	☐	☐	☐
4 I can get out and about without too many difficulties.	☐	☐	☐
5 I know why it matters to eat healthy food and manage to do so most of the time.	☐	☐	☐
6 I take part in physical activity at a moderate intensity (like a brisk walk) for 30 minutes at least five times a week. (Count anything that gets your heart rate up here!)	☐	☐	☐
7 I get out of the house at least once a day. (Walking to the corner shop to get unhealthy snacks doesn't count!)	☐	☐	☐

If you have answered:

- True to *all seven questions*, you're managing the Basics brilliantly. Skip this chapter and move on to Chapter 2.

- True to *four to six questions*, you're well on the road to noticing how important these things are to building resilience.

- True to *three or fewer questions*, this chapter might be really helpful to you. But don't give yourself a hard time about it. Just choose one thing from the list to try, even if it takes the whole year to sort!

Now you've answered these questions about the Basics in your own life, what about doing it with your child in mind? Fill in the Child Assessment Chart over the page.

What Basics does is to put the ordinary events and the practical things that go on in life into the spotlight, because they are truly significant. Believe us, making just one change is likely to have a knock-on effect on the others.

> It wasn't until I started walking the dog every day and seeing my friends a bit more that I began to feel a bit less miserable. I realized I was fed up with sleeping in the living room every night so I put finding a better flat, with two bedrooms this time, at the top of my list.

But how do you sort and do the Basics if it doesn't really float your boat? Well, hmmm, let's look at each one separately.

Enough money to live

Are you wishing money wasn't such a worry? Feeling broke or wanting the chance to earn more? Then unfortunately it's no doubt worth your while pausing and reading through this very tough potion. There are probably quite a few of you who are going to have to pause – just over 50% of families of children with disabilities in the UK are still living in or on the margins of poverty (see the CAF factsheet, and also Harrison and Wolley 2004).

No doubt about it, the job of raising children with extra needs is costly. If you're short of money it would be good to be honest with yourself and check that you're not buying your kids things they really

CHILD ASSESSMENT CHART

Child assessment	True	False	Sometimes
1 My child has a decent standard of living.	☐	☐	☐
2 My child has a place for their own things in our home.	☐	☐	☐
3 My child is safe and free from danger most of the time, I know where my child is most of the time and they have people who look out for their safety.	☐	☐	☐
4 My child gets out of the house at weekends.	☐	☐	☐
5 My child eats healthy food most of the time.	☐	☐	☐
6 My child exercises (moderate activity such as cycling, walking, playground activity) in some way for at least 60 minutes every day.	☐	☐	☐
7 My child has places to go to have fun.	☐	☐	☐
8 My child takes part in some social activity outside of school at least twice a week.	☐	☐	☐

don't need to make up for the fact that you don't spend enough time with them or feel guilty about something else. It's a common issue. But basic things like finding childcare, having extra laundry, buying specialist equipment or food and paying to get to endless appointments and meetings can be a real strain on the pocket. And having children who uncontrollably steal things or regularly damage property doesn't help either.

On top of all this, it might be really difficult to work. Lots of parents tell us they feel they don't have a choice and that it's often 'expected' they stay at home to care for their kids, even though they'd planned to be working outside the home.

You may find yourself going through a type of grieving process because having to give up work can mean losing your old identity or you may find there are greater expectations on you if you suddenly become the sole breadwinner.

> At work I had a job title, responsibility and people related to me as a colleague. Now I'm just a mum.

God knows many of us would jump at the chance to get away, even if it's for a few hours working in a boring old job.

DID YOU KNOW...

Depending on whether you have one or more disabled children, 11–16% of mothers and 51–63% of fathers are in the workforce – compared to 61% of mothers and 86% of fathers without a disabled child. (Russell 2003)

If you're one of the few parents who do manage to work because you have to or want to, finding out about ways of returning to work and any support available for working parents is worth the effort. Knowing your employment rights and being clear about any regulations, for example for flexible working and having time off to care for dependent children, is very important.

But even if work isn't a priority for you, chances are that maximizing your family income is. We both come from poor backgrounds where there wasn't enough money to go round. Kim remembers having a spell of having to raise her kids only on benefits. She ended up going back to work because she couldn't deal with the stress of getting into debt, even though it hurt heaps to leave her children. She couldn't afford proper stuff for her kids, for example she had a wonky pushchair and the wheel kept falling off every time she went downhill. The kids got really good at getting out of the pushchair and running off to get it. It's quite amusing looking back and thinking how we managed, but it wasn't funny at the time. Not having enough money is rubbish. We know it can make a big difference not only to your family's quality of life but to your own stress levels too.

So while you may not want or feel you need to, claiming any disability-related benefits you are entitled to can make a lot of sense. In the UK there are benefits designed especially to help families manage the extra demands of raising children with disabilities. And don't think you're not entitled because your child doesn't fit the traditional understanding of the word 'disability'. Look into it. We've both met parents whose kids are now teenagers who could have had the extra financial help all those years, but they didn't think they were eligible, were given poor advice or just couldn't face the forms. Millions of pounds aren't claimed. In the past, Angie herself missed out on £7000 because she couldn't face form filling. You could be awarded money that can really help with the practicalities and make life more manageable. And sometimes claiming these benefits brings other perks because often they're a route to extra allowances like free prescriptions, eye and dental care, concessions to activities, being able to apply for other sources of funding and so on.

We know that finding out what might be available, getting the right advice or help to fill in the forms can be bewildering. But if successful, it might be the best day's work you do. Having enough money coming in each week means you spend less time feeling worried about making ends meet. And for some parents it can mean affording the cost of getting out and about, keeping on top of repairs, buying labour-saving gadgets, children getting to go to clubs and activities and having extra tuition or therapies.

> We had a private occupational therapy assessment done and the report confirmed things we could see Asif was struggling with but until the assessment we didn't understand why or how to help him. Lots of her advice hasn't cost anything but it's really helped him at school.

> Because one of the boys is compulsive and the other one can't remember anything, they couldn't cope with proper cooking. Having a microwave was a safe way for them to sort their own snacks.

It's really weird how many of us leave filling in forms to the last minute. Some of us have ignored it altogether because it felt too depressing to focus on our child's shortcomings even though it meant losing money. So what helps parents to get on with making those claims?

Top Tips from parents – Claiming disability-related benefits

- Fill in just a few pages at a time – especially if you keep putting the forms in the drawer! It's better to take your time over it rather than put it off altogether.

- Write about a typically bad day – you have to make a case for why your child needs more help than others the same age and this can be a miserable task, so have a friend at hand to make those cups of tea.

- Get help from another parent with a child with similar difficulties – you can think about the sort of things that you should mention, together.

- Ask a friend without a child with special needs to help – it's easy to forget what other children of the same age can do for themselves.

- Look at any reports that professionals have written about your child – these can give you a clue to the underlying reasons your child is having difficulties and you can use some of their sentences.

- Don't worry so much about spelling and fancy sentences – it just has to be understood and able to be read by someone else.

- Think about the everyday events and how much you help with them – mealtimes, bathtimes, bedtimes, out shopping, using public transport.

- Get help – there may be organizations who can advise you or even provide someone to help fill in the forms with you.

(These tips are taken from an Amaze Factsheet 2008.)

Claiming benefits is just one aspect of having enough money to live. We know that, even if you do claim all your entitlement, you might still be feeling broke. Loads of parents tell us they have to budget carefully and struggle to make ends meet anyway because it costs more to have a child with complex needs.

And managing money successfully is quite a skill which doesn't come naturally to all of us. So if you're one of those people who find it hard to sort out your finances, remember that all kinds of people get into debt for lots of different reasons. But whatever the reason, there are steps you can take to deal with it. Most importantly, don't bury your head in the sand, because ignoring the problem will make things worse. Getting specialist debt advice needs to be your priority. There are organizations that advise on what to do and they can help with things like budgeting and applying for benefits and even negotiate with creditors on your behalf. Don't go it alone.

And what about working? While we don't want to diminish the vital and full-time job we undertake as parents, getting into paid employment can be a way of increasing the household income and raising our status in the world. But don't overlook the need to do the sums. Balancing the money coming in from working and what you're actually paying out in childcare might not make you much better off, well not immediately anyway.

I didn't go back to work because I had three little ones and nowhere could I find a childminder who would take all three.

But paid employment can help your own self-esteem by giving you a socially valued role and get you away from your kids for a while, if this is what you want. This may seem so far off for some, but if you do hope to return to work at some point, our advice would be to dip your toe in the water if you can. Volunteering, training or taking a job that maybe doesn't use all your talents are all ways of getting started and can lead to better things.

And before we finish talking about having enough money to live, and getting a good job, we know these are not always within our reach. Finding clever ways to make things happen or having an inventive approach to living on less might be your only option. Convincing yourself that 'less is more' might not come easily (it certainly doesn't to either of us), but there are ways of making a little go a long way.

Good enough housing

A warm, cosy place that you look forward to coming back to at night? A welcoming kitchen that you love pottering about in making your kids their favourite dinner? Enough room for your child to get in and out of the bathroom in their wheelchair? Does this sound like your house? If so, skip this section. If not, read on because we all need a decent place to live. The business of living and housing involves a great deal more effort for many of us compared with families of children who don't have complex needs. Working on getting a decent home environment might take a long while, but it is a very resilient move.

If only it was as simple as keeping them warm in the winter.

Just sorting enough space can be key. Having room to play at home when our children are less likely to be invited out as often as others, or can't use parks and communal spaces without our help, can make daily living much more manageable. Gardens and outdoors are a favourite place for most children, so if you're lucky enough to have an outdoor space it can make a big difference making it accessible and safe. Not being able to move about easily because spaces are small or rooms feel cluttered and cramped can get in the way of making everyday events manageable and hassle free. Not having enough space to fit wheelchairs or walking frames can have a knock-on effect on children getting the exercise or therapy they need. We can underestimate the impact of our housing on our family lives. Particularly if you have a child with learning or behavioural difficulties, lack of physical space can create tricky issues for everyone managing to get away from each other. Having somewhere to go on your own without other people around can provide a refuge to ponder in, paint your nails, read the newspaper and a safe space to calm down to boot.

Getting our home right has really helped us both to cope.

Brothers and sisters need their own personal space too. Sharing a bedroom with a child who wakes frequently during the night or destroys their belongings can lead to war. If your home is a difficult place for your children to live in, finding ways to make it safer or more accessible might be a real priority for you.

I've put locks on the bedroom doors for now so when we're not in them, we lock them up. Sounds awful I know but he just can't help his compulsive stealing and I've tried everything. I need to know my stuff is safe and his sister needs to know it as well.

I saved up the money and used it to make the garden safe.

It just never occurred to me that having carpets and soft furnishings would make such a difference to the noise levels for my daughter who wears hearing aids.

Lots of parents tell us their housing is unsuitable and that this has made caring for their children harder. It's contributed to them feeling stressed so getting good information and advice about your housing options, including the possibility of adaptations, is vital.

If your home needs to be adapted, be warned, the public housing system and schemes to adapt homes for disabled children can be difficult to understand. And the process is nearly always time consuming and frustrating. So it makes sense not to wait until your situation is risky and you are at breaking point before you investigate the options and ask for help. Again, remember it's often good to enlist someone when things seem beyond you. Getting good advice is your first step.

And if you rent from the private market, it's likely to be even more difficult to make your home safe and accessible. Sometimes it just isn't possible, reasonable or practical to adapt a property and the best option is to move to a place with more potential.

While there is value in living in a neighbourhood of your choice, it can make sense to give some thought to the things that matter to you when researching the neighbourhood to move to. Kim remembers living in a street that made her feel sad. She moved to a cheaper part of town to get out of debt but noticed after a while that her quality of life had deteriorated in other ways. She felt isolated, there were no local shops, the bus service was poor and it didn't feel safe for her children to play out without her. While we all have to compromise at times, think about which bits matter most to you.

But what if you can't do anything about it? For example, if you live right next door to a pub where people are outside smoking, drinking, talking or arguing? Or if you've got the most popular street in town for teenagers to congregate because they haven't got anywhere else to go? And what if you're on the local authority housing list with little power to do much about moving anyway?

If making changes for the better looks unlikely at the moment, you may have to be persistent and hang onto your hope that things will improve one day. You may have to work with what you've got. Doing a few little things around the home to brighten it up might be the best available option to you at present. Make your home a bit of a sanctuary somehow.

> Someone told me to buy myself a bunch of flowers every week and it really worked – I've done it ever since.

Look for the little things you can do and do them. And it pays to keep up with repairs if you can. Whether your child has kicked in the door or shredded the wallpaper off the walls, if you live in an uncared-for environment, you're likely to feel less valued. But get the balance right for yourself. If you need to have things tidy and clean, fine. But being house-proud might not be your top priority. Leaving the washing up and going out sounds like a resilient move to us.

I remember when my daughter dropped a bottle of something in the bathroom and it ended up in the loo and cracked the toilet bowl. I had no money to replace it for weeks. The garden got com-posted though!

It's quite interesting talking to kids about their home. You only have to ask a few children about the places they live to know which bits really matter to them. As a parent you might be most concerned about safety and the risk that some areas of your home present such as the stairs or bathroom. Obviously, you'll know the toll it has on you if you have to lift and handle children up and down stairs several times a day, so sorting a way to ease this will be a clear priority for everyone. But for children, they might be most concerned about being able to use the kitchen so they can prepare their own drinks and snacks.

I love the smell of cooking and when it's all been tidied up and clean.

The best bit about my home as a kid was living near to the sea, because in the summer Dad would get back from work and we'd immediately go for a dip together.

I'd love to have a chair right up in front of the television so my nose touches the screen.

Now, we wouldn't recommend rearranging the furniture to suit kids' unhealthy viewing preferences, but it is worth asking them what they think. The smaller things can make a surprising difference to how happy and comfortable your children feel at home.

Being safe

It's easy to imagine the world is a dangerous place. Especially if your child's experience so far has been that others stare, tease or bully them because of their difference. But we should start this section by explaining that the world isn't any more dangerous for kids than it was many years ago. It's just that our perception has changed, and the media can make out that the world is dodgier than it actually is. Facing up to what might seem to be dangerous can in fact be a learning experience for kids, as Angie found out when her daughter went missing one day – she had nipped out to offer an alcoholic homeless man her pocket money, which he politely declined.

But all this is easy for us to say, and might not calm you or your child down. Growing up and learning is risky business often because there's a chance we might fail. So safety is really important. If a child is anxious or afraid to be out of your sight, or worried they'll be hurt, they will naturally try to avoid the situation and won't want to learn new things that will help them to grow. This is a developmental issue. It's fine for tots to be clingy – in fact it's not a healthy sign if they're all over total strangers. But as children grow up, it's normal for them to develop independence. For children with complex needs this can be especially difficult, so you'll have to help them. In fact, you may have to look at your own behaviour. Are you cocooning your child too much?

Children need to move out of their comfort zone and learn to do things that are beyond what they can already do, otherwise they'll have trouble developing to their potential. So it's a bit of a balancing act for us, trying to provide enough safety whilst also allowing room for taking a few risks. Being safe is about helping children to let go of having you around all the time and learning to manage the risks of being in the big wide world.

WHAT MAKES A SITUATION SAFE FOR YOUR CHILD?

See if you can list a few ideas here:

We can exhaust ourselves thinking we're the only people who can help our children learn to negotiate the world successfully. So using people like grandparents, aunts and uncles and close friends known to your child, to provide safe places for them to experience the world without the comfort of you around, can be a great place to start. Their first time away from home or their first sleep-over at a relative's or friend's place can be a gentle way of helping them to know the world can be a safe environment.

> When I get a babysitter, I do the dinner but leave the bath bit on purpose. He learns that other people can do these things and not just me. In the beginning, I thought it wasn't worth it because of the kick back when I got home, but I thought stick with it, stick with it — we've got over that now.

But it can feel like a really big step leaving your child in someone else's care. After all, you're putting your trust in people who you might not know, like school teachers and play workers. So it probably makes sense when you can, to meet with people beforehand if you or they don't know them. Depending on what it is of course, it might also make sense, to be clear about what you're expecting of them. We're thinking here of those times when you're choosing a childminder or leaving your child at an after-school club, for example. See if you recognize any of these top 'preparation' tips we've collected from other parents.

Preparing to meet new people and do new things

- Don't rely on what it says on the can! Publicity materials don't always show what it's really like so find out for yourself. Is the atmosphere a happy one and does this new person make an attempt to connect with your child?

- Make a visit before you leave them on their own. Take your child along so everyone can get to know each other.

- Ask other parents and other children for their views about the person or place but be careful about believing rumours.

- Use what you do at home as a yardstick. While you probably can't expect others to do the same, it's reasonable that it at least fits okay with your way.

- Encourage your child to talk about the new person or place because what matters to them might be different to what matters to you.

- Don't be worried to ask if they have any experience of your child's type of difficulties. Even if they don't you'll want to know they're interested and willing to find out more.

- Expect hiccups. Even when everything seems okay there are often teething problems while everyone adjusts to the change. Give it a chance.

(These tips are taken from an Amaze Factsheet 2008.)

We realize it can feel like a tightrope for parents sometimes. Pushing children to try things out when they're ever so anxious might put them off trying anything at all. But wrapping them in cotton wool doesn't do them any favours either. And taking too laid back a view about what they do and where they go can leave them unboundaried and vulnerable.

As strange as it might sound to some, children can gain lots from being exposed to negative experiences. Angie and Derek call this 'inoculated resilience' in their original RT book (Hart and Blincow with Thomas 2007). Children learn from bad situations, like the first time they enter the pool without their safety arm bands. They get to feel the fear and do it anyway. Finding the positives in bad situations is usually a very resilient approach to take.

But of course there is a balance to be struck. Planning for risky situations with them and going over things afterwards to spot what went well and what they could do differently next time can reassure you as well as your child.

> We agreed I'd ring once she got to the cinema but we hadn't counted on her mobile being out of signal. I managed to get hold of her friend but next time we rehearsed how to find and use a public phone and she had to ring me.

Children need to know you are supervising them and, for some of us, our kids are going to know that it's dangerous to let them out of our sight. But if you're lucky enough to have a child you can allow to go off on their own, or who gets invited to the occasional sleep-over, making yourself ring them and telling them they have to be back by a certain time is important. Because there's no getting away from it, you need an eagle eye as they learn to spread their wings, even if they resist it at every move, and you're so glad to see the back of them for five minutes! Research tells us that it is worth checking up on them because it communicates to them that you care where they are, even if it seems like they don't notice, or it makes them more cross with you.

It takes some doing to get the right approach, but we can't rely on our kids to know themselves how to respond appropriately. Sometimes children need help to learn how to notice the early warning signs, like the way their bodies respond when they don't feel safe. You could try talking this through with them. Did they notice, for example, how clammy their hands were when that lady smacked her dog in the supermarket? Perhaps they were worried she might lash out at them? And what about the time a man shouted strange things at them in the street? Did that give them butterflies in their tummy?

Dealing with any sort of aggression, like being bullied at school, being picked on at the park or managing violence in the streets, is horrible. Most of us have at some time in our lives known what it is to be in a hostile situation or be on the receiving end of someone else's scary anger. So we know it hurts and can make us miserable. And it can feel even worse if it happens to our children.

DID YOU KNOW...

Children with disabilities and special educational needs are more at risk of being bullied than other children. (Facts on bullying can be downloaded from the following sites: Mencap; NAS; and CAF – see the Resources section. See also Batten 2006.)

We've got a few ideas that might help children deal with aggression. The first is quite simple: problem-solve with them. You could get some more ideas on this from Chapter 4, Coping. There is nothing so awful we can't talk about it. Showing your child you want to listen to them can make a big difference. They need to be reassured that telling you is the right thing to do, that you won't get too angry or upset, and that you will support them. Helping them to think about ways they can deal with difficult situations to see if they can come up with ideas themselves to feel safe is a very resilient thing to do. And asking them what they would like you to do helps too.

Second, having a network of people children can turn to, and knowing how to spot safe people for help if they need to, is a resilient move. There's more in Chapter 2, Belonging, about this.

Third, one of the very practical things you can do in the moment is to think of ways to build their confidence. Spending extra time doing things they like and with people who like them is an obvious one. And don't rule out introducing them to new things so they get absorbed in something fresh.

> Having ADHD meant he did lash out and so I looked into all the different martial arts. Karate gave him a good discipline. It's a defensive and not an attack one. And for the other one who is withdrawn, he used it to block an attack when he was bullied at school. And it keeps them fit of course.

So martial arts is one hobby your child could develop that would help them in many ways. Let's take a look at other things they might do in their free time.

Play and leisure opportunities

Play and free time is an essential part of growing up for all children. There's not much research on this, but we do know that access to open spaces, free play and leisure opportunities helps improve young people's wellbeing. It enriches their development in all sorts of ways – socially, physically, intellectually, culturally and emotionally. They learn to understand themselves, other people and the wider world. Getting out and about gives them the chance to feel familiar with their neighbourhoods and good about their communities. And our hunch is that it makes parents feel better too.

So why have we included it in RT when it's what all kids do naturally? You probably know the answer. Children managing challenges and difficulties in their lives often don't get enough access to play and leisure.

Just imagine what it would be like to wake up tomorrow to discover your child's been invited to three different parties, has single-handedly baked the birthday cakes, bought the presents, got themselves dressed and worked out how to get there! Or imagine another parent rings you to tell you what an exceptional child you have and would they please come over and play again. Let's face it, children with complex needs don't get invited to much and some of what they get invited to is really rubbish anyway. And the reality is, sorting play and leisure with and for your children probably means becoming their 'social secretaries' for a long while.

Finding things for them to do can take quite a bit of extra effort because you want to know they are safe and supported wherever they're out playing or enjoying themselves. But you might have to take account of the barriers too.

Things like a lack of physical space at clubs or no adapted play equipment, inexperienced workers or the receptionist's attitude are a real obstacle. Added to these, a lack of time, money or transport, arranging extra supervision, the threat of bullying or neighbourhoods feeling unsafe can all get in the way of us making play and free time work well for our kids. But we reckon hurdles are for jumping and barriers are for getting around and knocking down. Just because a club or activity hasn't done it before doesn't mean it can't do it now. And just because you've had a knock back before doesn't mean you give up. You've got to be prepared to shop around and try things out. Sometimes it's just that particular worker, or that session in the week, or that the helper was off sick, that explains why the first try didn't work.

So finding out what's available in your area might be your first port of call. It's worth checking out what's on offer regularly as things change according to the seasons, holiday periods and demand. In our area, there are clubs and organized activities for almost everything, including activities that everyone uses and a few specialist clubs and sessions that are just for children with complex needs or disabilities.

Asking your child what they want to do might help to narrow things down. See what they come up with, without you influencing their choices or encouraging them to do what you think is best. And keep an open mind because they may want to distance themselves from special activities because they want to be like their friends who don't have any impairments. Other children, of course, may feel easier when they're with children who seem more like them. The bottom line is you want to know they're happy, having fun and are welcome. Parents with children with similar needs to yours can be a good source of information about safe places to go and fun things to do.

Joining a club is another useful way of helping children to make new friends and discover new interests in a safe space. But we probably don't need to tell you that you'll have to do some careful hunting to find what suits and works for your child. And if they're reluctant to try anything or show little interest in your suggestions, you might have to be a bit cunning and introduce things through the back door. And remember, organized activities aren't the be all and end all for every child. It's more about getting out and about and doing things that matters.

> When we go for family picnics I choose a spot on top of the hill, so the kids have to go a bit further.

> We have a video competition in our house. Whoever does the most push-ups gets to choose what we watch.

Don't give up if whatever they're interested in isn't your passion or they only have one love and that's computers. Go with it because you can always encourage other things too, so that they have the opportunity to explore all of their talents and interests.

Chances are you'll have lots of questions when visiting new possibilities and you'll be itching to hear reassuring answers. You know, those 'what if' and 'how will you' type questions. But it can be a bit of a balancing act getting the essential information sorted so you can stop worrying and not put a club off or make them lose their confidence about trying to include your child. Maybe watching how a session runs could give you more information anyway.

Joining a new club can be daunting for everyone and it can feel especially scary for kids who have trouble making themselves understood or making sense of new situations. And for workers, meeting a child for the first time, with needs you've not come across before, can make people feel a bit nervous. So it's a good idea to have at hand a few helpful things you and your child want everyone to know so you all feel okay. Decide beforehand if you prefer to only explain your child's differences on a 'need to know' basis or ask them to think about how they would like to be introduced and whether they'd like to do this themselves.

It might also be worth remembering to try to do some things as a family because it's easy to concentrate too much on your special child and get the balance wrong. We mention this with an added 'health warning' because we're also aware that we can get too ambitious. Bear in mind you're not 'The Waltons' and planning a family holiday away for two weeks without any television might be a tad unrealistic. However, if you do want to do more together and your child's needs make it hard to fit in with ordinary family stuff, joining up with other families who have children with similar needs to yours for days out or afternoons in the park can help you feel more relaxed and confident about it all.

And while we're talking about being too ambitious, we reckon it's also okay to let opportunities go. When a child needs a lot of extra help to play and learn, it can be hard to resist the urge to say yes to everything that comes along. But action-packed days can be exhausting and stressful for everyone. Not every moment of the day has to be filled with something educational. Children need time and space just to be themselves and to daydream.

> I make sure he has a mental health day now and then. He has the whole day off just pottering around at home, catching up with himself.

If you ask children and young people what matters, they just want to have fun, usually with friends. So while play and learning aren't separate and very much linked to children's all-round development, it's easy to get hooked up on rules, structure and learning outcomes. These may be important too, but not at the cost of having a good time.

Sometimes creating fun opportunities for your child might simply mean making your home a place for play. You don't have to always be thinking of clubs and activities outside the home. After all, play is what children and young people do when they follow their own ideas and interests, in their own way and for their own reasons. They don't have to be with others to do it.

> You don't need fancy toys and the latest gadgets. I used to put together a 'making' box – full of old loo rolls, sticky bits, glue and stuff. And then they could do what they liked with it, I just made sure I had put new stuff in it and stayed out of the way.

> My kids have had hours of fun in the garden with a simple hose. And they liked it even better when I said they could keep their socks on.

> I remember Krishna having a whole day's fun with just a couple of old cardboard boxes. While she would call out for help occasionally, the trick was to let her alone.

And finally, here's the thing: when was the last time you had some free time, tried something out that was fun or simply played? Exactly – we can get so caught up with being responsible and sorting our children's lives that we forget how to play and enjoy things ourselves. You might need a break. If this isn't easy to admit without feeling guilty, remember it can give the rest of the family a break from you too!

Having somewhere safe to go and something to do is part of the business of building a child's resilience because it's about increasing their skills, confidence and self-esteem. And our guess is it's an important part of your survival skills too.

Exercise and fresh air

When you think about exercise, you're probably like us and picture swimming, football, running and working out in the gym on a treadmill or lifting weights. And depending on your relationship to all this, the words that come to mind might range from no way, yuk, dreary and boring right through to hard work, good idea, fun and brilliant. While you might want to notice if any of these get close to your own response, what we'd like to suggest is that you forget all that for a minute. Suspend your own ideas about exercise. Because for children, exercise is usually much more straightforward and can often mean simply playing and being physically active.

Some of the ideas we included in the last section are relevant here, but it doesn't have to be organized sports or dedicated, separate activities. Instead, it can be part of the routine things they do in their daily lives, like going to the park, exploring the world around them, playing at home, dancing to the latest music or getting from A to B under their own steam. Playing outside or walking to school may be all that your child needs to increase their exercise levels.

DID YOU KNOW...

Walking and playing provide children with more physical activity than most other activities, and these activities are really good for kids. (Mackett 2004)

But how much exercise should kids get? The Chief Medical Officer for England advises that children should achieve a total of at least 60 minutes of at least moderate intensity physical activity each day. This means any activity where your child is slightly out of breath and slightly sweaty. So while it's only a minimum recommendation, it doesn't have to be a taxing exercise where they're so breathless they can't talk to you, although you may well prefer this at times! Nor does it mean doing a whole hour's exercise all at once. It can be broken down into two or three smaller, easier chunks over the day.

If you're confident your child is already getting enough exercise and fresh air and they're already meeting this minimum requirement, you might want to skip over this section. For the rest of us, who find it quite challenging getting our children to exercise, take comfort now, you are not alone. Most children in the UK are not getting enough exercise. The latest health survey for England found that three out of ten boys and four out of ten girls are not meeting the recommended hour a day (Department of Health 2004).

Somehow, we seem to have a lifestyle that doesn't involve much physical activity any more. When we look back at our own childhoods, we can't remember being driven to school and, if it was too far to walk, we got ourselves to the bus stop. Kim's Australian and recalls her school days being about swimming club and netball games and after school looking forward to mowing the grass, mucking about in the creek, building hide outs in the bush or running up and down the hill to get the best speed out of the go kart. Angie, on the other hand, was a little more constricted by the soggy English weather and asthma but she still rushed around on her bike.

Children today seem to be opting to spend more of their time doing inactive things like playing on their computer games, texting on their mobiles or watching TV.

DID YOU KNOW...

A recent poll conducted in the UK found that British children spend an average of 5 hours and 20 minutes a day in front of a TV or computer screen. (ChildWise 2007)

We can't assume, then, that children are naturally active or that it's easy to get them fit. Plus there are extra barriers for children with complex needs to manage. Apart from any limitations caused by their impairment, we're thinking here of things like limited outdoor facilities or parks that are accessible and safe, children needing extra help to take part, sports and recreational facilities that are hard to get to or too expensive to use, lack of understanding of the ways of adapting activities to meet the needs of different children, fear of being excluded and lack of role models or supportive adults to make exercise fun and appealing.

Consulting the resilience evidence base can help to keep us on track. Regular exercise can be brilliant for children in more ways than you might think. Check this out. It lowers their risk of heart disease. Research has shown that people who have a physically active lifestyle are at approximately half the risk of heart disease as those who don't. It can improve their mood because it stimulates the chemical serotonin which makes us feel happier and less stressed. So it's good for managing depression and anxiety. It's a natural pain relief because it triggers endorphins, which are anti-stress hormones that block pain signals in your brain. And muscles get defined, body fat melts away and skin glows, so it can improve their confidence because they look better!

And we've not finished yet. It's also a chance to meet up with friends or make new ones, forget about the stresses of school and even build a sense of achievement as they discover talents they never knew they had. And if you're a professional reading this book, you're probably already familiar with the research that promotes sports and other physical activities as distractions for young people at risk of involvement in crime. Exercise is a great way of burning up adrenalin and can help control anger before it gets out of hand. In a nutshell, kids who are physically fit are better able to handle everyday challenges. And when it's all too much for them, or for you, being fit helps them to sleep better too.

So any activity that gets children more active can only be good. But here's the thing, your child getting fit probably depends on you. You may prefer not to know this, but studies have shown that sedentary and inactive parents tend to have sedentary children, whereas active parents have active children. Hmmm, well we're not mentioning it to make you feel guilty or angry because we know it's difficult teaching ourselves to enjoy being active, let alone getting our children to join in. Kim's the sort of person who used to stop exercising the minute she started perspiring! But if the thought of exercise doesn't make you jump for joy or you think you're rubbish at it, all the more reason to tackle things from a resilient angle now. However hopeless you think you are, there are things you can do and there's a physical activity out there that will suit you, and your child. You've just got to make a commitment to change and find it.

The truth of the matter is, you are in a prime position to model a healthy lifestyle, and you never know, your enthusiasm for a new-found physical activity just might rub off. The trick is to find ways to make it fun so that we and our children manage to do it regularly. Little and often can often be the answer. Like taking the stairs instead of the escalators or lift, getting them to help with weeding the garden or washing the car, walking the longer route home or leaving the car in the furthest corner of the supermarket car park. Every little bit helps and, if these little things get built into your daily routine, no one will even notice it's exercise.

If you want to help your child to make some changes find something they enjoy. While walking is definitely one of the easiest and cheapest forms of exercise, it might not be on the top of your child's list of fun things to do, unless you make it into an expedition or a hunting game, of course. Children often try to be like their friends or relatives and will copy them. So ask someone they like or admire to join you for a walk because the moment they are out with friends, they forget they're walking.

Some children will respond well to setting targets and tracking their physical activity level each day, like using a pedometer to measure how many steps they've taken. Others will be less interested and one of the best ways of getting them to be more energetic is to limit the amount of couch potato time they spend doing things like watching TV or playing computer or video games.

> We decided to push an activity habit into them from the start. We kept them ignorant for as long as we could! We didn't want them knowing about the other options until it couldn't be avoided. Of course, once they got to school they were right there with the rest of them, wanting gizmos and mobile phones.

> Chantelle spends hours on that trampoline. It's the best thing we ever got.

> My boys go to special needs football, Scouts and kick-boxing. They need very structured activities with clear rules. They aren't good at occupying themselves and they need to know where they stand. With three of them, it means a lot of running about but it's all good.

> We didn't know anything about yoga. Thought it was some mystic twaddle. But we tried it and it's perfect because it's just for kids and she gets too tired for most sports.

Choosing something they enjoy, making it part of their social life, going at their own pace, varying the routine, setting achievable goals and making exercise a habit are all good tips for keeping up with an active routine. And giving some thought to whether your child is likely to prefer competitive or non-competitive activities, or individual, group or team opportunities, can also be worth thinking about. And don't forget, make sure they drink enough water.

DID YOU KNOW...

Lots of children are dehydrated and those under 11 should drink approximately a litre of water a day. But more if they play sport or exercise a lot. (Expert Group on Hydration 2006)

Between 50 and 60% of our total body mass is made up from water and on a normal day we lose between two and three litres and even more when we exercise and sweat hard! So it's up to us to replace it every day in order to keep our bodies functioning well. Apparently we can cope without food for quite a while but going without water for just two to three days will lead to serious health problems due to dehydration.

And before we finish this section, what about you? Are you getting enough exercise and fresh air? The recommendation for adults is at least 30 minutes of at least moderate intensity at least five times a week (Department of Health 2004). Notice all the 'at leasts'. You've just got to keep reminding yourself that it's worth it, because you are the one who will benefit.

DID YOU KNOW...

90% of people report a boost in self-esteem and wellbeing after a country stroll. (Mind 2007)

Without doubt, exercising can be a powerful way to build resilience. We've already said that it lowers our risk of disease and major health conditions, helps us manage our weight, improves our mood and confidence, provides natural pain relief and can help us to live longer. And getting regular fresh air can really blow the cobwebs away.

> Many a time I've felt this downward spiral of misery and hopelessness come over me and as long as I remember to get out of the house, walk a few streets and notice the bigger world, I'm okay.

So once you've got over worrying about looking ridiculous or getting sweaty, keep focused on all the positives. How you present yourself to the world can really help build your resilience. And listen to this – apparently exercise makes us feel good because it stimulates feel-good hormones, and once you've been exercising regularly (for about six months), you'll be so used to this good feeling that you'll miss it if you don't keep it up. We can't decide if getting hooked is a good thing or not! As long as you avoid getting obsessive about it and don't forget to give your body time to recover you're probably on the right track. Even if you eat rubbish food, a bit of exercise will still help.

Resilient therapists are interested in energizing children to take charge of their health and exercise more. But you've got to look after your own activity levels as well. How about trying one thing out – you're in a key position to jump start change for the better. Do your best.

Getting about

The last section will have given you a few ideas about how to kick start an exercise routine, and the one before that some play and leisure opportunities. Exercise, play and leisure often means getting you and your children out of the house. But some activities can be quite some way away, and quite a challenge to get to – unless you want to include a ten-mile walk in your exercise routine every time your child wants to go to their martial arts lesson. One of the priority things disabled teenagers say they would like to change in their lives would be to get out and about more easily (Murray 2002). Being stuck at home is soul destroying and can result in serious depression. We don't know from the research quite what the picture is for parents of children with a bigger range of complex needs, but our own experiences and those of parents we know show us that getting out of the house can be a challenge. Taking part in the wider world is, in itself, a resilient mechanism. It gives families opportunities to expand their horizons, discover new talents and socialize with other people, and all of this relies on being able to get out and about.

Although there's not a great deal to say about getting out and about that's not obvious, we've included this short section because it's often an area that gets overlooked. Professionals, for example, don't always understand how hard it is for the families they are working with to get to appointments – they need an inequalities imagination to do this. You might need to gently point out to them that you need help with getting places. Not all professionals are as understanding as this one Angie once interviewed for a research study she was doing:

> For a minute I was sitting there feeling angry that my client hadn't turned up, but then I thought better. I got here this morning in my nice car. But if I had to struggle down the road in this rain with a double buggy, get two different buses and then walk all the way from the bus stop with three kids hanging off me, only to get here and be nagged by two do-gooders, maybe I'd just say stay home and stick the television on.

Travelling with children can be hard work. You may not be living anywhere that's easily reachable. It can be exhausting, emotionally draining and expensive. So it's worth exploring the help that might be available to make getting out and about more manageable.

If you don't have a car and travelling on public transport with your child is not possible, ask whether you can get an ambulance, hospital car or help with taxi fares. Speak to the hospital social worker or consultant.

> I invested in driving lessons. I could see we weren't ever going to be able to manage a holiday away but at least now we can go for days out.

> After school we always get the bus out to the big park before we go home. In the holidays, we get on trains and travel all over the country. I used to say 'no': it was money we didn't have. But now I can afford it and the trips make him so happy, I think I've begun to enjoy them almost as much as he does.

Another fairly obvious tip is to find out if someone else is going your way, and arrange to travel with them. At best they'll have a classy sports car, but even if you end up having to go on the bus together it could make the journey more bearable.

We mentioned the idea of a ten-mile walk to get to martial arts lessons earlier on. And we were joking when we said it. But it is worth thinking about whether walking or cycling is possible. Investing in a good pair of trainers might help make a four-mile round trip seem bearable and think of how fit you'd get if you did that regularly. And don't forget, bikes are a great form of transport and another way of exercising!

> We've bought an adapted tandem bike. It's a funny looking thing but she loves whizzing around on the front of it. I pedal and steer from behind. So now we all go out cycling together, the others on their own bikes, Dad in front, and the two of us gathering up the stragglers. It's a real laugh!

And now a word about public transport. Of course there's the general difficulty of frequency and lack of buses and trains in many places, with rural areas especially challenging to live in because of this. For physically disabled children using public transport can be a real bind, but even where public transport is accessible to wheelchair users, other disabilities may not be considered. Young deaf people are just one group who have unequal access to public transport. For example, announcements at train stations are clearly inaccessible and this can lead to losing your confidence travelling alone and limiting independence. You probably won't be surprised to learn that a recent study by the Disability Rights Commission found out that twice as many young disabled people said they lacked confidence using public transport than their non-disabled peers (Disability Rights Commission 2003).

But what if you do have the best bus and train service in the country with lots of adjustments for disabled people? Children with complex needs will still need a lot more help getting their heads around how to use them than will their peers. For many of our kids it really isn't practical for them to use buses and trains on their own until well into their teenage years, if at all. But some of you might be lucky to have a child you could let loose a bit from the age of 11 or 12. Take a good look at yourself and decide if you really are being over-cautious.

A study carried out in schools and colleges on transport discovered that many disabled young people seldom use buses or trains because their parents were too afraid to let their children learn how to use public transport on their own, as they thought that there were too many dangers (Finch *et al.* 2001).

Even if you can't let them out on their own for a long while yet, it's worth getting them to join in with planning routes, using bus and train timetables, buying tickets and noticing where they're going from a young age. This kind of active involvement lays the foundation for eventual independence. Letting them take the lead on planning and carrying out a journey, with you travelling alongside them, but not organizing things, can be a really helpful stepping stone towards travelling alone one day. Hard work for you we know. But if you take a long-term view it could be worth it.

Healthy diet

Right now, you might be thinking 'you must be joking, of course my kids need a healthy diet, but easier said than done'. So this is the point when we should blow the whistle and tell you we are two fat ladies who struggle with our own diets and exercise. We're waddling proof of how hard it can be to take note of the importance of basic things like healthy eating and exercise.

But it's impossible to focus on getting the basics right and ignore mentioning diet and the foods we eat. However, it is truly very hard to say exactly what that diet should be or how you get children to eat it. We're all individuals with likes and dislikes and very particular circumstances and lifestyles that have a bearing on what healthy eating might mean for each of us. So it's just not realistic to expect all children to happily have one diet that works for each of them. And we can't and don't want to prescribe specific diets or tell you what to feed your children.

But we do know that food is very important to their wellbeing. It affects their moods, behaviours and their ability to learn. It's not hard to think of times when different foods left us or our children feeling happy and relaxed, sad, uncomfortable, tired, manic and even guilty.

> If I don't collect him from school with a snack in my hand, I know I've got problems – he'll kick off before we get halfway home.

RT is interested in pin-pointing the little things we can do in our everyday eating patterns to encourage children to eat the foods that help them to bounce back. Luckily, the research offers a few useful pointers.

Just as we now know that alcohol and caffeine have been proven to seriously affect our moods, it just might be that other foods have an effect too. So it's worth checking it out. For example, we know it makes sense to limit foods like coffee, tea, cola drinks and chocolate because of the caffeine. And there are foods that are worth including like Omega 3 which is found in oily fish and vitamins and minerals which have all been shown to have positive effects. But how strong the effect is depends on the individual and their circumstances. For example, people with specific conditions like depression and nutrient deficiencies seem to benefit the most. And while some vitamin supplements can help with mental health problems, vitamins mixed with prescribed medications from the GP can create problems, so it makes sense to be careful and seek advice. There are a number of specialist groups offering very specific advice on diet for children with a range of complex needs. For example, support groups for children with Attention-Deficit Hyperactivity Disorder (ADHD), dyslexia, irritable bowel syndrome and autistic spectrum disorders come immediately to mind. If you're thinking about supplementing your child's diet it makes sense to get some advice.

Providing food for our children is often a big part of us feeling like good enough parents. So the examples we set with our own eating habits can have quite an impact because children's eating habits are often 'programmed' in at an early age. And, interestingly, none of our children are fat, so this proves that you can help them, even if you find it hard to help yourself.

You will already know that taking a variety of foods from the four main food groups – bread, cereals and potatoes; fruit and vegetables; meat, fish and alternatives; milk and dairy foods – makes up a balanced diet. And you'll know that sugars and fats are also a vital part of a balanced diet, but only needed in very small amounts. But maybe having a picture of these food groups and what portions to ideally eat, posted clearly in the kitchen, would be a way to remind everyone about healthy eating.

DID YOU KNOW...

The daily recommendation is to eat at least five portions of a variety of fruit and vegetables each day – on average in the UK, we eat less than three.

The daily recommendation is to eat a maximum of 6 grams of salt a day – on average in the UK, we eat 9–12 grams. (Department of Health 2005; Food Standards Agency 2006)

You might be thinking we're flogging a dead horse now, because you've already tried umpteen ways of improving things in your home. No doubt about it, making changes probably means persevering and not giving up at the first hurdle, even if that hurdle looks too high and too familiar. If you're struggling to get good habits going, you might find making just one of these small changes will set you in the right direction.

Ideas for improving eating habits

- Get what you put in your shopping trolley, or in your food cupboards or even on your dinner plate at home, to match the picture of the food groups and the ideal portions.

- Don't have sugary foods like cakes and fatty foods like crisps in the home. Replace them with starchy slow-energy release foods like nuts and seeds, wholegrain snacks like muesli bars, homemade flapjacks, vegetables like carrot sticks, breadsticks, peanut butter, fruit and yoghurt.

- Choose wholegrain rather than refined white cereal products.

- Avoid foods with colourings and additives as these are linked to hyperactivity, and sweeteners in diet drinks and cordials are linked to behaviour and mood changes.

- Choose healthier plant oils like sunflower or olive instead of saturated and trans fats such as vegetable shortening, hard margarine, butter, palm and coconut oils. Unfortunately, these bad oils are often in cakes, biscuits and ready-made meals so you can be eating them without realizing it.

- Eat oily fish like fresh tuna, salmon, mackerel, pilchards, trout and sardines twice a week or, if your child's vegetarian, eat seeds and dark green vegetables and you could use linseed oil in salads.

- Choose fresh ingredients and cook simple meals as much as possible.

- Get your children involved in cooking so that they don't rely on fast food.

- If you find it hard to get your kids to eat vegetables, puree them into a sauce.

- Cut down on salt in cooking by using herbs, garlic, chilli, ginger and spices instead.

- And getting enough fluid (not fizzy drinks or alcohol!) into our bodies also matters.

It's not just what we eat, it's *when* we eat that's important too. For lots of us, just getting everyone to eat together is a major challenge. And you might have already exhausted ways of making family mealtimes enjoyable. Like getting your children to help cook or setting the table interestingly, or making up some games while you eat. While the ideal might be to have a family rule that the evening meal happens together, this might not be realistic all the time. Having a few nights of the week when this happens, with the TV off, might be enough. Because, don't forget, you need to look after your own diet and have a quiet time yourself to eat a nutritious and enjoyable meal without interruption sometimes. Or if this is not for you, at least make sure you have a nice lunch occasionally, while the children are at school.

Having a child who's a poor or picky eater, or who overeats and is constantly hungry, can create all sorts of tensions in a household. No doubt about it, you might have to be incredibly creative and flexible while you try to encourage new eating habits.

> My son really restricts his diet and he sits down at the table and says he doesn't like it even though he ate it last week. So we made a menu with him. He said he liked pasta, rice and noodles. So then we did the thing about there being no vegetables and fruit, so he had to decide what to put on his menu from these other food groups.

It can be slow progress, so make sure you notice any little advances. If you're just starting out, we found that choosing a few things that seem achievable and are more likely to work is a better place to begin. For example, you might want a rule that fresh water is for mealtimes and sweet drinks are only for special occasions. But you want to make that fresh water look its best with an ice cube or a straw at least! Or you might need to hold your breath and resolve not to have sweet drinks in the house at all. The kids might kick up a fuss and go thirsty for a few meals, but fingers crossed they'll settle down after a while and get used to it.

Simple things like setting a rule that everyone sits down while they eat could be a stepping stone to getting fidgety children to eventually sit down at the table. Or offering smaller portions and gradually increasing their size might be a more realistic way to get the reluctant eater to finish off their plate. You could even slowly add something new to the plate alongside the things they've already agreed to eat. Or if it's hard to get your kids to eat vegetables, puree them into a sauce. Landmark research by Leann Birch indicates that offering a child a new taste, a couple of times a week, up to ten times, should help them develop an acceptance or liking for it. Apparently the foods kids taste most often, even if they just spit it out at first, are the ones they will most prefer, so it's worth persist-ing (Birch 1982). Cutting food up can work a treat for children who find it a bother to eat. A whole orange is not as appealing as one cut up into smaller portions to eat with a toothpick and a kitchen towel for those children who can't stand messy fingers. And cooking together can make it harder to resist eating it.

Some children have trouble knowing when they're hungry or thirsty. So you might want them to ask first before helping themselves, so that you can check out whether they're eating because they're hungry or because they're bored or worried. Or for children who overeat, you might want to keep the cakes and biscuits out of sight, or better still, don't have them in the home at all. Only have basic nourishing food like fruit and bread available. Having predictable mealtimes is another way to help children manage their anxieties about food. Interestingly, research indicates that how our food looks, smells and feels is very important to us and can have a much greater effect on our mood and behaviour than the way it tastes. So cutting the toast into fingers ready to dunk into the boiled egg is more significant than you might have thought!

Healthy eating for children can drastically improve their mood and behaviour. But putting a decent meal on the table is just part of the story. More often than not, we find ourselves having to learn to manage worrying eating habits and poor diets with little interest and often full-blown resistance from the children we want to help. So you have to be creative, dig deep for that touch of craftiness, anticipate small steps and be prepared to be flexible.

Conclusion

All children ought to be able to rely on the kind of basic things in life that we've considered in this chapter. We hope to have convinced you that it's important not to miss the significance of ordinary things like these, when we're busy working to promote children's resilience.

But we're aware that the ground we've covered in this chapter makes for quite a daunting list. So where to start? Going back to the child assessment at the beginning of this chapter might help you to break it down into manageable chunks. Children need the basics in place to give them a head start and support their development. And we reckon you do too, which is why we've added the following checklist – have a go.

RT BASICS CHECKLIST

	Yes	No	Sometimes
I give myself a little money to spend on myself.	☐	☐	☐
I have a space in the home that is just for me and my things.	☐	☐	☐
I do something to pamper or take care of myself weekly.	☐	☐	☐
I make sure I get out of the house each day – even if it's to get a pint of milk!	☐	☐	☐
I treat myself with healthy food and drink when I can.	☐	☐	☐
I've found a nice way to exercise throughout the week.	☐	☐	☐
I do something enjoyable during the week.	☐	☐	☐

Well, have you got the *basics* in place for yourself? If the answer is yes, move onto the next chapter. If the answer is no or sometimes, before you go on, make a deal with yourself to build up just one of the things from the list. Which will it be? Remember, you're worth the bother.

Let's recap

Basics – this potion conjures up the basic necessities needed for life.

- Enough money to live.
- Good enough housing.
- Being safe.
- Play and leisure opportunities.
- Exercise and fresh air.
- Access to transport.
- Healthy diet.

CHAPTER 2

BELONGING

Introduction

> I would never have thought I'd end up feeling at home round a table in Antonio's Pizzeria on my daughter's birthday with such a motley crew. Me, my ex, and current partner, a whole load of quirky teenagers spilling food down their fronts and waving at the waiters and a picture of the dog out on the table. It makes me chuckle to think about it.

Everyone needs to feel they belong. Even though we are each an individual, we need to belong to groups, however informal, that accept us. Whether it's family, friends, school mates, work colleagues, even the place we live, it's the way we create our sense of ourselves, our identity. It's a basic part of being human and very strong in us all. Families like ours can achieve belonging in our own unique style.

Some researchers reckon belonging is the most important aspect to resilience building, and everything else you might try to do pales into insignificance. We don't go that far, because we've seen for ourselves that some children really struggle to belong anywhere at all and yet there are things that can be done to build their resilience none the less.

The resilience literature makes it very clear that if you have a lot of good relationships, or at least more than one, then it will help you to manage life resiliently. Everyone longs to feel cared for, so building and keeping successful relationships can really help children to feel good about themselves. If they can be kept going over time, and you can be hopeful about the potential to build new ones, so much the better. If you can tap into good influences, enlist the help of others and focus on the good times, your children's capacity to respond to challenges will improve.

For children who develop ordinarily, and live at home with their birth parents, good early bonding provides a safe and dependable base. Professionals call this 'attachment'. From this they learn to explore and play, cope with uncertainty and take risks. When children experience care and containment, love and safety at an early age, they develop the idea that the world is a relatively safe place and they can slowly let go of the apron strings. So from here they bounce off to build on their sense of belonging as they opt in and out of various groups and establish different kinds of relationships throughout their lives.

But first and foremost, ideally children need to feel valued and loved at home, by you! If you're in the tricky position of feeling that you often struggle to do this, don't despair. This is a taboo that we feel comfortable to face up to, and hope that you can too. And in this chapter, we don't take it for granted that you unconditionally love and value your child, but at the same time invite you to work on how you manage your responsibilities, and work towards some form of loving relationship. This is a tall order we know. That's partly why there are so many remedies in this potion. Take heart, there are a lot of ideas to draw on. What resilient researchers and RT have done is pinpointed the aspects of relationships that are significant to building a child's sense of belonging. We've summarized the evidence base into 12 remedies:

1. Find somewhere for the child to belong.

2. Help a child understand their place in the world.

3. Tap into good influences.

4. Keep relationships going.

5. The more healthy relationships the better.

6. Take what you can from any relationships where there is some hope.

7. Get together people the child can count on.

8. Belonging involves responsibilities and obligations too.

9. Focus on good times and places.

10. Make sense of where a child has come from.

11. Predict a good experience of someone/something new.

12. Help a child make friends and mix with other children.

We'll be getting on to exploring the remedies in detail. But before that, let's take a moment for you to take stock of your family and where you belong in relation to other people – we'll come on to a sense of place, and even contact with animals (of whatever breed), later on! You could do the next 'Relationship Web' exercise thinking about yourself, or if you like, do it with one of your children in mind. Play around with it.

By noticing which relationships are not helpful, as well as the good ones, you can begin to make decisions about where to put your effort. We realize this isn't black or white, and no relationship is perfect, but clearly some relationships have very little going for them at all, and the best thing we could do is get rid of them. When we asked a few parents to experiment with this exercise they gave us some interesting feedback.

> It made me sad and angry because I couldn't really add my family. But at least it pulled into relief that I have to give my other relationships more attention – there's not enough people on my web.

> I put Ben's taxi driver on the outside at first. But he is so significant to our lives – he turns up on time every morning with a cheery smile. It helps us start the day well especially as he hates going to school. It made me rethink how I might take care of that relationship a bit more.

> I actually did a circle for my son. He started off saying he has no friends, and it's true he doesn't have peer group friends at all. But I got him to talk about all the people he cared about and who was there and what did they do and all the rest. And he drew a page full of people. He was surprised – for him to actually sit down and look

RELATIONSHIP WEB

Draw a bull's eye, like the one illustrated, on a large piece of paper to map out your current network of relationships.

Think of all the people in your life – for example, family members, friends, acquaintances, and other people, like paid helpers, for example! Now plot them on the circle according to how important they are to your life – for example, if there are individuals you feel close to or are really significant to you (maybe family members, maybe not), place them close to you in the centre of the circle. Then add those people who are in your network but are less important to you towards the outer part of the circle.

Once you've mapped out the web, take a moment to ponder what you see:

- Are there any surprises?
- Who's central to your web?
- Does it make you think of people you should spend more time with?
- Are you putting lots of energy into relationships that aren't very helpful?

at all these other people that he had relationships with, was really very special for him. A lot of them are Mummy's friends but they are also people who will spend time with him. And it only took 20 minutes.

Find somewhere for your child to belong

Sharon goes to Rainbows and loves it. She really feels part of the group. And Toby, he loves going to his Nan and Grandad's house because he feels comfortable there.

> ## DID YOU KNOW...
>
> The Social Issues Research Centre conducted a poll in 2007 with over 2200 UK residents on the theme of belonging:
> * 88% said family was the key marker of belonging.
> * 65% said friendship was an essential part of their sense of belonging. (SIRC 2007)

Forming a strong emotional bond, or 'attachment', is a normal biological process which helps to protect children during those vulnerable early years of life. What's interesting, and a bit overwhelming at times if you think about it too much, is that attachment depends largely on the way we as parents behave. For a baby to become securely attached, they have to be confident that we will respond more or less consistently to their needs. (Although remember what Dr Donald Winnicott said about 'being a good enough parent' and not a perfect one.) Still, it does mean we have to be pretty much always available to them, when they are tiny at least. No wonder we kiss goodbye to a good night's sleep and there's a weight of responsibility associated with being a parent from the word go!

Attachments usually happen by the time babies reach the age of three and we create the bonds without even realizing it. So the quality of what we offer in those first few years is crucial. For example, babies who have no option but to attach to neglectful and abusive parents, because that's all that's around, usually struggle to have proper relationships in life because they don't have good foundations on which to build. And this is why helping mothers who are managing postnatal depression to be loving, responsive, consistent and predictable is such a seriously important task.

And while it's quite risky saying it here, it's just possible that some children born with disabilities or complex needs miss out a little on the instant bonding, particularly if their parents have had no warning or preparation. Sometimes the shock or disappointment of having a child with impairment or illness and the reactions of others can get in the way of us attaching as quickly as we might have liked. For some foster and adoptive parents it can be equally hard to develop deep and long-lasting connections with their child.

The good news is that we do know children can do well even if they haven't had that early nurturing care, and there's always something that can be done to improve a child's sense of belonging.

So while it makes sense to start with this at home, there are lots of other forms of belonging that should be worked on too. Some children with complex needs mess up good relationships and connections ever so frequently and easily, so it's worth having a few different places that your child feels at home, at the same time. It's a bit of an insurance policy.

> John loved the Beavers and liked going off in his uniform each week. But he took some cigarettes in, and ended up blowing it there. At least he's still got our local park that he feels at home in, and pops down to most days after school. I notice how he gently sways back and forth on 'his' swing. He still sneaks a few cigarettes when I'm not looking, but at least he can't be chucked out of the park for it.

Put simply, children need somewhere to call home, and we don't just mean the address, although actual buildings matter too. So this remedy is quite simple. Boiled down it's about relentlessly looking for places they can belong, to feel a part of. This could be connected to their gender (a girls club for example), their culture or ethnicity (like a specialist black young people's project), or tapping into a talent or interest (sports clubs perhaps). The bottom line is this is a place they can return to when they've been rejected elsewhere, and life seems really tough.

> Yeah, belonging. My son Rasheed must be the only 19-year-old who feels at home in the Thomas the Tank Engine official fan club. But whatever floats your boat.

Help your child to understand their place in the world

We don't see how we can help children with complex needs to understand and decide their place in the world, without also considering their relationship to being part of a minority group. Of course, groupings like gender, ethnicity, sexuality and race are important when boosting resilience too, and we bear them in mind. But we're focusing on disability because our book is for parents of children with complex needs.

Current estimates (see EDCM 2007) suggest that 5–7% of the UK's children are disabled and one in ten children are reported to be struggling with mental health problems. While you might not be thinking of your child as belonging to a minority group, the chances are that others are. We know that thinking about what this might mean for your child might raise strong responses or painful feelings, but we're going there anyway because we think it's important.

Let's start with ourselves – usually, a very good place to start! Can you spot which one of these parents is most likely to be the parent of a child with complex needs?

Spot the difference

Unlike some of our children, there are no tell-tale signs that you've entered a different club. You probably blend in with all the other parents, apart from having darker bags under your eyes! It's possible that you've had very little opportunity to think about and reflect on where you are yourself with having a child with complex needs.

If this is the case, we'd like to recommend you avoid falling into the trap of what many describe as following the 'medical model' of disability. This is where children are seen as faulty, diagnosed and labelled, and their impairment becomes the focus of attention while their ordinary needs are put on the back burner. Specialist assessments and services take over.

We notice that parents benefit from and prefer to put the following resilient spin on things. Your child is a child first with strengths and qualities like the rest of us. But they also have needs that are helpful to define in order to sort the extra support they require to reach good outcomes. Thinking like this means you take a more 'social model' approach to their disability. You value and welcome their diversity, noticing that relationships are crucial and expecting to have some information and training yourself, about how to support their needs.

This is the time to draw on that inequalities imagination we mentioned at the beginning of Chapter 1, Basics, because an approach that communicates your child's right to basic services and normal human respect will rub off on them – and those around them.

It's also good to think about whether or not, or how, you want to refer to your child's difficulties, understanding and then framing for yourselves how they relate to the wider world. It can help you feel more in control and you get to manage situations and the reactions of others, rather than feeling that bad things just happen to you. There are some very strongly held views about this and the pros and cons of having a formal diagnosis.

Some say labels can be stigmatizing and lead to people assuming the diagnosis involves certain problems when it doesn't. We've all seen people speak over loudly and slowly to wheelchair users, when their only impairment is to do with their mobility. And sometimes a diagnosis can give the impression that things are static, change is impossible and that children won't be able to manage or respond to ordinary events and so they don't get offered them. Or ordinary problems can get overlooked because people presume that every ache, pain or tricky behaviour is just part and parcel of their condition.

On the other hand, some say that naming the impairment or disability acknowledges that a child has real problems. It helps explain symptoms, behaviours and difficulties and avoids children getting wrongly labelled as bad, lazy or naughty. It can also help others appreciate how hard it might be for a child to manage certain things easily, so they anticipate the need for extra help and encouragement in advance. And of course, having a diagnosis can often provide useful information about what can help. Lots of parents tell us that having a diagnosis has been the gateway to extra resources.

> It's all very well for the medical professionals to say you don't need a label but the education system demands one to release the services.

> Labels can be a foundation. Get it and put it away in a drawer. Don't stick it on until you need it.

Of course, it's important for parents and professionals to understand the diagnosis but it's also important for children to have a line on it too. For children who struggle to understand their diagnosis, you'll have to chat it through, and keep coming back to the conversation to build understanding. Check out what your child makes of their diagnosis. Angie overheard this conversation between 14-year-old Jane and 11-year-old Brian.

> Jane: *Yeah, you've got OTT, does that mean you've got a specialist dysfunction disorder too? A small brain like me?*
>
> Brian: *Yeah, but my brain's a bit bigger and I keep washing my hands all the time.*

Children notice other people's comments and are often very good at detecting moods and how others feel. Given society in general has a rather negative attitude to difference, complex needs and disability and that we're all exposed to these unhelpful ideas and representations, it's likely that our children are picking up parts of these harmful messages too. Once people believe the diagnosis is a bad thing, it's ever so easy for this message to be unintentionally passed onto our kids. If this happens, they're in danger of becoming resigned to their situation and they might give up trying or lower their own expectations. So it's worth using the ideas in this book to find ways of managing any disappointment or sadness you may have.

RT is interested in finding ways to strengthen children so that the effects of prejudice are reduced. Think back to the idea of 'inoculated' resilience that we mentioned in the last chapter. Children can be helped to use their so-called past 'bad' experiences to their advantage. You can encourage them to transfer the learning from hard times to new situations. Angie says that growing up in a household where her parents were always fretting about whether or not they could afford the rent, and thinking they'd be kicked out any time, had its advantages. It made her vow to get her own house, and she put huge efforts into getting onto the property ladder.

> I heard a worker tell Ali, ADHD is like a throwback to the days of hunting, making him all alert and ready for the kill. He said to him that because we're not in the wild now, when he takes his Ritalin at school, it makes him calm so he can fit in with everyone else. But his friend who is calm all the time can't ever be like a hunter because he can't move between the two. It was great, he basically told Ali he was lucky because he could switch and others couldn't.

Tricky things that might have caused our children real distress can be turned on their heads. And you and your child might also want to consider the benefit of joining up with families in the same boat as you. Apart from loads of parents telling us that other parents are the best source of information, they also say it's really helped them to feel less isolated.

For children, hanging out with other children, young people and even adults managing similar situations can help develop a sense of identity and belonging. It can support the strain caused by those who have trouble accepting and appreciating difference. It can help them to integrate their experiences of impairment with the way they come to understand their place in the world.

The issue about children's relationship to their disability is too involved for us to do justice to here. For example, we know from Tom Shakespeare's research (an authority on issues of 'disability' and a disabled role model), and the work done by Ruth Marchant with disabled children, that many disabled people and children don't like to be identified as 'disabled' (Marchant 2008; Shakespeare 2006). The reasons are complex but one of the things children have said is that they get no street cred from the label. On the other hand, the organization Kim works for has developed the Compass Leisure Scheme, where disabled children get a discount card for swimming and the cinema and some children are very positive about their difference.

> My son says to his mates, 'We can use my discount card. You can't have one because I'm special.'

In the meantime, experience tells us that finding ways of coping with prejudice and discrimination can set children with complex needs (and their families) on a resilient path. Sure, you may have to grow a tough skin in the process.

One way of supporting children to manage tricky situations is to help them see that they are not alone and not the only ones managing difficulties. Use some of the ideas we offered in the 'Being safe' section of the Basics chapter.

> I tell my son he is CYBORG (like the character in Star Trek) and he loves it.

> I use the strengths of her impairment – she has brilliant visual memory.

I turn to his specialness. I remind him he has no fear of trying new things out.

Decide if you prefer to only explain your child's differences on a 'need to know' basis. Would it help, for example, if the local shopkeeper understood their needs and why? Having to hand a few helpful things you or they want others to know to smooth the way might be worthwhile.

When the time is right, try talking with them about their diagnosis or difficulties and seek their views on how to present this information to the world around them. It's important to give children the chance to understand themselves and their abilities and how their impairment, illness or diagnosis impacts on them. After all, they're the ones living with it. In much the same way as we might explain the hormonal changes to a young person coping with adolescence so they understand why they might be having such radical mood swings, so too might it help to explain what's involved in a diagnosis. Pitching all this so that it matches your child's age and developmental ability is, of course, as we have said elsewhere, really important.

Apart from keeping a sense of humour and finding other things in life that give you pleasure, having a few phrases or ways of talking about difficult issues at the tip of your tongue to ease awkward situations can help. We call these 'cover stories'. People can have a real knack of putting us in situations that can almost force us to have to respond. Here are a few examples we've collected from parents to illustrate what we mean.

He just says to people, 'I'm a bit too energetic sometimes. That's what ADHD is.'

He has a learning difficulty, he can't help it, but you can.

I hate it when people tutt and huff or give me the evil eye. One man even said to me, 'Can't you control your son?' I turned to him and said, 'Actually, I'm really struggling, can you give me some advice?'

Sometimes you can't talk your way out of situations and people will be downright abusive and insensitive. Here are some ideas from parents about what they do in those situations.

- Walk away.

- Remember that the person saying these things is probably deeply sad and lonely.

- Decide not to let it touch you and don't engage with the issue.

- Say what you need in the moment and just keep repeating it.

- Debrief with a friend.

- Give yourself a really special treat.

- Allow yourself to get upset.

- Disarm people by agreeing with them.

Unfortunately there's no magic cure for people being nasty. With a resilient mindset, you can help your kids to work it out and decide their place in the world based on the positive things and not the negative around them.

The people who mind don't matter, and the people who matter don't mind.

Tapping into good influences

We mentioned in the section about finding somewhere for a child to belong that their earliest relationship with their parent or primary caregiver in the first few years of their lives lays the foundation for their sense of belonging. But the notion of attachment to one positive adult is a western concept. We know there are tribal systems and kinship models in other parts of the world that share parenting and provide alternative models for helping a child to know they belong. Whole villages and communities assume the 'European' role of relatives for children and create powerful bonds linking children into networks of relationships that meet this basic need.

For those children who haven't had their 'attachment' needs met by their parents, others can go some way to meeting them – but of course, it's not so easy to establish when it's not the way things are traditionally done in the west. We reckon many of you would be pleased to share the load a little and would welcome others into your families with open arms, if they wanted to take a genuine interest in your kids. Tapping into good influences is about identifying and encouraging others to take a role in your child's life. Look back to your relationship web at the beginning of this chapter to see if you had hardly anyone on it. Is it possible that it's because your family is really unpopular, or because you don't want to let other people in, or you think you're the only one who can handle them?

Finding others is easier said than done we know. But remember the ideas in the noble truth of enlisting mentioned in the introduction. Having a few extra role models for your children can provide them with support and back-up in addition to what you offer. They might be people your child already knows like teachers, club organizers and school secretaries, or they might be people you seek out or 'friend up'. What these people have in common is that they act in ways which show your child good and acceptable ways of being with others. They demonstrate how to do and say things and, because they're liked or looked up to by your child, they imitate them. Ideally they are the sort of people who model honest and decent ways of being in the world and can even introduce them to new activities and values. Most of us can recall how important certain people were in our childhoods because they believed in us or gave us that extra bit of attention or guidance. We should never underestimate the impact on a child's life of a caring adult who is able to be there for them, even if only for a short while.

> There's a school helper who always makes a point of telling the children not to shout at each other. She's like a broken record. But because he likes her, he remembers it. I make sure I tell her she's liked because I want her to keep teaching him these things.

There are groups that can provide this sense of community and acceptance and are a good influence – like churches, clubs, community and cultural groups or groups that meet to share common interests like the Scouts, music and drama groups and so on. They are all potential places for your child to develop their sense of belonging. And, they can play an important role in giving children extra attention, and in helping them to learn to trust others.

Keeping relationships going

It's hard to stick with children when they have loads of difficulties or they behave in ways that don't exactly endear them to us. Setting up and maintaining long-term relationships that see kids through different stages of their development can be difficult.

It's important though, because long-termers are more likely to understand your child's needs and care about and invest in them. We don't mean financially (although we wouldn't object), we mean giving them their time. When children get to know and feel comfortable with people (which for lots of our kids takes time and perseverance) they can relax and worry less about getting on with others, shifting their energy to more exciting things.

A shame really that social care and health organizations often fail to prioritize continuity of relationships. Therapists and social workers seem to move on and change so frequently. Just when it seems like a miracle has happened and you get someone useful – the next minute they're gone and a new worker, who your child doesn't know, turns up.

So how do you pull off continuity of relationships? Well, working with and through those people who know your child the best and who are likely to be around for a while could be a good place to start. Who would that be in your child's life?

Let's think about people on your home ground. Moving house happens much more frequently than it used to, so knowing who's likely to stick around can be a bit of a guessing game. Having a sense of local community is still important to our idea of belonging, but it's more to do with the place where we live now rather than where we were born. However, you can still keep relationships going even when people have moved away. Little things like remembering to send birthday cards can communicate caring and concern that provide a real sense of history for children.

Or joining clubs and organizations can offer a sense of membership and belonging without having to rely on one interested individual. These days it's more common for children to belong to a number of groups rather than just one and, while this makes it easier to join and leave, it can be hard for children to be uprooted. Given it can take our kids longer to forge relationships, and they don't often have the same leisure opportunities as others, moving about too much can mean they miss out on feeling a part of something. Identifying those clubs and organizations that are stable, well known and dependable might be worth considering. It's also worth honing in on those clubs that will let your 13-year-old stay on beyond the ten-year-old cut off, because she's developmentally much younger. Clubs like Scouts, gym and Woodcraft Folk have branches all over the UK so they're a particularly good way to help children to put down roots in new places.

Children need people in their lives who will commit to them and accept their situations. But lots of people don't want to know our kids because they're nervous or haven't any experience of how to handle their quirky and challenging ways. Leave a few copies of this book hanging around and they'll soon get some ideas! But you will still have to fill them in on your own child's weird and wonderful ways.

Prioritize relationships with people who have seen your child through difficult situations. It's likely that they will be more understanding of some of the things your child has had to manage in the past. Invite them along to school events and birthdays, because celebrating progress with others, however insignificant it can seem, can build your child's self-esteem. Of course, you might have to orchestrate them all yourself, but there's a pay-off if your child gets the message that they matter enough for others to celebrate and mark occasions for them. You could comfort yourself by thinking how nice it will be when your child fondly remembers these occasions ten years down the line. And don't be afraid to contact these significant people to ask them to get in touch with your child if something bad is going on. Children need to know someone is interested in them, especially when the chips are down.

If you end up being the only source of continuity for your child, try to expand their networks, but in the meantime think about those little things you can do to communicate continuity and reliability. For example, you might have a few rituals that can help you to achieve at least a degree of stability of relationships without too much effort. Texting your child, timing it to arrive just when they're on their way home from school each day, is one idea. Shame you can't pre-programme your mobile to do it for you! Funny little household customs, like Friday night family DVD night or Tuesday toasted sandwich night, all count. These rituals are useful ways of keeping relationships going.

The more healthy relationships the better

Children with complex needs are likely to experience their fair share of negative relationships. The disapproving 'tut tuts' from passers by in the street, the low expectations of some professionals and the bullying and teasing by their peers are just a few examples of what they have to contend with.

This remedy is all about increasing the number of good influences in your child's life, so they outweigh the bad ones! Your aim here is to do what you can to make the healthy relationships stronger and more influential than the negative ones, even if you can't shift the crap. So here goes.

Suggestion number 1: Get animals involved

> Who would have thought that getting a dog would change our lives so much! It's Jake's responsibility to look after her and so he walks her every day and people stop him to comment on how lovely she is. My son now has a network of dog walkers that he calls his friends.

> Sian's not very popular in school so I did other things. We started with horse riding so she could build up a relationship with the horse! Not people to start with – too hard.

The point here is that you don't have to only rely on people – go hunting for some animals! Children are often attracted to animals because they are uncomplicated, straightforward and honest. There are even some schemes that actually use dogs to help children recover from traumas. Animals don't keep secrets, they don't tell you off, and they don't make fun of you.

Encourage your kids to have a pet, or if you really can't face that, adopt an animal to visit occasionally at the local rescue centre. Kim can't understand the sentiments of dog lovers herself, but she tries really hard to respect their feelings when the dogs are sick or die. There's no point encouraging your child to have a pet if you can't find it in yourself to praise your children for the relationships they develop with them.

Suggestion number 2: Managing nightmare friends

> When my kids like someone and I know they're not good value, I keep them close – the ones we don't like. I get my kids to invite them out with us on family events because, if they like you, they're less likely to do anything bad to your kids. I build a relationship with them in the hope that they'll then be less likely to cause hurt.

> The only kids who'll come around are the other kids with difficulties. So we built up a relationship with another family who had a child at the same time without any problems. If we parents hadn't wanted to be friends, it wouldn't have happened.

In an ideal world your child wouldn't be friends with all those kids who drive you mad, but… One tip is to steer a course between letting them have these troublesome friends, and cutting them dead. Allow occasional calls with strict time limits (you don't have to tell your child that landline calls are free from your phone). Keep times they spend together short, a two-hour tea is much more manageable than a 12-hour sleep-over.

Suggestion number 3: Let the sunshine in

> Some people are just sunshine most always – they make it seem like good weather even when it's pelting it down.

Make sure you have friendly, cheery folk that you can't help but like around you. We all, it is hoped, know how it feels to be in the company of positive people – how their optimism is infectious. Once you get one in your life, recognize it, celebrate their sunny personality and stick to them like a limpet. It's one of the more enjoyable things we can do for our children.

Suggestion number 4: Keep your eyes open

> Sometimes I thought I was having no effect keeping on telling him to ring me as soon as he got to his friend's house, when half the time he didn't bother, but it must have helped him to feel that I cared about where he was.

Think back to the being safe remedy we mentioned in the Basics chapter. Closely supervising your child builds resilience. It might not ensure your child hangs out with the right crowd, but it effectively gives them the message that you care.

Suggestion number 5: Out of little acorns…

> Lucy loves popping down to the local takeaway every Friday night. She has a good old chat with Dillon the bloke who's been serving her for the past four years.

Our children's relationships don't all have to be deep and meaningful. Lower-key ones can have a good effect, and together they can seem quite significant. We mean those consistent contacts – with clubs like Brownies, but also with the local shopkeeper, the neighbours – people who have been around for a while and are likely to be around for a while longer.

Take what you can from any relationships where there is some hope

This remedy helps us to exploit the positive in any of our child's relationships, even ones that feel rather rubbish. But it can mean that you have to think in quite a generous way. If someone disappointed your child in the past it doesn't always follow that they will continue to do so – people can change. Also, an adult who was unhelpful to your child when they were two might be better relating to them at the age of eight. For example, we know birth parents who badly neglected their very young children, and yet are able to provide more positive input now their child is older and sorting their basic needs is out of the way.

So this remedy encourages us to rethink our networks. While you might need to take a leap of faith to believe that there is potential in relationships that seem quite negative, it's worth giving a go if you want to take up every opportunity to positively expand your child's network.

MATCHMAKING

Think about the people you know who could maybe take a role in your child's life, even if at first you reckon they're a bit of a waste of space. For example: wider family members like aunts and uncles, cousins; people from your network of friends; parents you've met through your child's school; neighbours, and so on. Choose five and write each of their names at the top of one of these squares:

As you think about each of these people, list a few of their interests or skills (if they've got any; if not, abandon the exercise and treat yourself to a chocolate biscuit – God knows we consumed enough of them writing this book).

Do any of these match your child's interests? Could these be a way into developing a relationship between them and your child?

Seeing things from another person's angle can provide new opportunities worth making the most of. Have a crack at this...

> Even though I hate my ex-husband's guts I put up with him because I know that Jenny loves mountain biking with him.

Get together people your child can count on

This remedy overlaps a lot with tapping into good influences, but the idea here is that you get these people connected up to each other. This might be actually face to face, or simply that you, or someone else, has to co-ordinate their input. Call on the noble truth of enlisting.

So why do they need to get together? First, in everyday parenting, research emphasizes the importance of shared values and compatible parenting styles for children. It can be enough of a struggle for two parents to agree on how to tackle things when they see each other every day. Imagine how much harder it can be if those parents don't live together! Helping other people involved in supporting your child present a united front will mean that you'll need to communicate across the network. Even when you don't agree, appearing as a united front to a child matters. The situations children with complex needs are managing will demand more effort from you. Whoever is involved, you might want them to follow the same ideas we've offered in this book. Perhaps you could hand it on to them when you've finished!

Often co-ordination will fall at your door, or you'll end up doing it by default because the so-called lead professional isn't managing to do the job properly. But before you take on all the work, think about using other people to help with this role. It can take a lot of time to get people talking to each other and sharing information.

Belonging involves responsibilities and obligations too

Giving and taking is almost like the glue of family life, keeping links between each of its members. Properly belonging involves understanding the joys and challenges of relationships, and putting some effort into it. Children nowadays don't always know much about this, and sometimes are given, and expect, everything on a plate. Having relationships is not just about taking, it's about giving too.

It's good to start children off on a path that sees responsibility and obligation as a central part of belonging. Children who have appropriate roles and responsibilities including errands and odd jobs have a good chance of developing positive self-esteem and a sense of being able to make their own mark on what happens in the world. For our kids, we need to find responsibilities and obligations that are developmentally appropriate. And watch out for cultural, historical and gender differences in what we might expect them to do. Angie remembers having to do more housework as a girl, while her brothers mended the bikes. The balance is a fine one – think about whether it's fair for your child to be doing what you've asked them to do.

Here are some ideas you might like to try:

1. Encourage children to take part in community group activities that aim to do some kind of good deed – charity runs, clearing up the school playground, painting the community centre.

2. Have a pet and make your child their primary carer rather than you. Borrow one first and try out caring for it for a day or two, because pets aren't just for Christmas.

3. Get them to remember birthdays and special occasions and make cards for people they care about. If this is too ambitious have a handy stash of cheap cards in your drawer that they can use, so at least they send something.

4. Give them little leadership roles. Home light bulb changing monitor, head bin emptier or school register runner might sound rubbish to us, but to a five-year-old (or when it comes to some of our kids, at 15), they can seem like very grand responsibilities indeed.

Focus on good times and places

With so much distress and difficulty in our children's lives, it makes sense to highlight and bottle the good times. Looking back can then serve as helpful reminders for children especially when things feel a bit grim. It can cheer them up.

Remember we talked earlier about developing rituals, family customs and ceremonies. These are not only helpful in the moment. They serve as a record of good events that have happened and you can revisit them in later years. They're a reminder that, despite the difficult things, there are lots of good things too that shouldn't get buried under the misery.

Bottling good experiences can help children reconnect to people in their lives who have had some degree of healthy relationship with them. It can contribute to a collection of positive family stories – ideal for looking back and reminiscing.

One idea is to keep a family photograph file – look at it sometimes and talk with your child about all the people, recalling what was happening and musing over the funny events of the past.

Making time to be together can be hard but it is one of the most important things you can give your child. Finding even a short space in the week when you make sure you won't be distracted, so that you can give your child undivided attention, will reap rewards.

It gets easier, though, if you establish routines that work for you both. Like reading together at bedtime, having a slot on Saturday mornings to do something nice together, or simple things like collecting the Sunday papers together from the shops, having ten minutes after evening meals to play a board game you played as a child or briefly practise a musical instrument together. These things work best when they're regular because then the routine becomes expected, can be looked forward to and provides a structure that helps children to feel safe and secure.

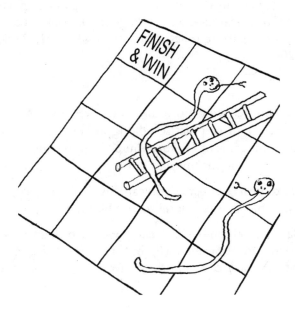

Sam wanted to know, okay, what is the payoff having a kid like him? And I was having a bit of a bad day, and said, 'I don't know, let me get back to you.' But then we had a lovely chat and I told him it's those times when he's had a really good day at school, and he tells me about it and he's happy about it and he's excited — it makes me feel good. And when he smiles…

Make sense of where your child has come from

We don't mean explain the birds and bees here! We mean, help them understand their history. Most children we have in mind as we write this book would have had a fairly up and down route to get to where they are at the moment. Helping them understand their history, sharing stories with trusted adults and children, builds resilience. It develops connections and a shared account of things. In the stories that they tell about their own past, parents and other adults can show themselves to be valuable role models for children, demonstrating how they managed life events and change. We cover this a bit in Chapter 5, Core Self, too.

DID YOU KNOW…

25% of all families in England and Wales are single parent units. However, of those families with a long-standing illness or disability, 32% are single parent units. (Barnes *et al.* 2002; Buckner and Yeandle 2006)

For all those children who no longer, or never, lived with both their parents, it's important to practise talking about their different households and how this came to be. For some situations children need a cover story, and we talked about this earlier on.

You need to be as honest as you can. Alcohol can make you sick and I say it hurt me, it was painful to see him that way.

Their dad is Portuguese and, since we have been to visit, they're more Portuguese! Sounds silly but it's enriched them — they are much more aware of it and they have a bigger connection with it now.

Their daily lives are about being brothers – I would never say they were half-brothers. It's really important that sense of belonging – the grandparents have them both, they don't split them either.

Predict a good experience of someone or something new

This remedy is about getting rid of defensive ways and putting more trust in others. It complements maximizing healthy relationships – when you get one going well you can use it as a springboard to develop others.

Predicting a good experience involves setting something up to look good even before it has happened. For example, persuading your child to come along to a picnic, telling her she will have a good time and that she will meet lots of people who will enjoy playing football too. Of course this involves a bit of a risk for you, as it might fall flat on its face. So you will need to put some effort in to make it work. Anticipate and plan for things to go well. For example, you will need to have a good enough knowledge of what will happen at the picnic and may need to brief others about their role in supporting your child when she's there.

Accompanying children on their visit to a new club or event is really important. Telling them precisely what is involved can help them to take the risk and go. And for those who are really struggling, the pain, fear and rejection may still be countered with the tentative thrill of broadening horizons. Try to persuade them that the results will be worth it. Give them a safety net by telling them you are trying it out and they can leave after 15 minutes if it's not fun.

For those children who are very anxious about attending anything new, worry about meeting new people or don't show much interest in doing things, you could have a stab at this exercise. It might help you think about ways of breaking things down into smaller steps that are less scary for them.

ONE STEP AT A TIME...

1. Think of a structured group activity (like swimming lessons) that your child might attend.

2. Think of an activity where your child could do something in pairs, just with one other person, but with some adult supervision.

3. Think of a group activity that has adult supervision.

4. Think of a semi-structured group activity that has less adult supervision (like Scouts, sports club).

5. Fantasize about each of these with your child, focusing on what will be good about them.

Helping children to take the risk and try new things requires loads of flexibility on your part: plan it, do it, quiz it – to see if you can identify what works well and not so well.

Help your child make friends and mix with other children

The whole realm of making good friends and mixing well with other children does not come easy to our children. Their drive to find some sense of belonging with children of their own age can lead them to develop negative peer relationships. And as they get older, research shows that this does little to build their resilience. But this is all easy to say, what can we do about it?

For our children's sake, you could try being fairly open-minded about what counts as friendship. We often think a friend needs to be someone the same age as our child. But our children can make good friendships with people who are very different ages to them because they are not so influenced by societal norms, and developmentally they often function at a different age to their chronological one. Children's ideas about friendships develop as they get older. It's usual for children in the first few years of school to only have a few friends. They don't get more choosy about their mates until they're a bit older, maybe not until they reach about nine years old. Look back at the child development stages in the introduction to get an idea of how kids often begin to make more effort to develop a network when they're a little older.

> His brother was three years younger, so he borrows his brother's friends.

Even though your child might have quite a few negative relationships in their life, forming just one positive relationship can be powerful. Dr Michael Rutter's (1989) research on young women growing up in a children's home is interesting here. He found that those young women who went on to marry a decent man did much better. (We're more used to hearing people say that all a struggling man needs is the love of a good woman, but Rutter's research concluded the opposite!)

An alternative approach is to get as many relationships going as you can. This means that, if one goes wrong, at least there will be others to compensate.

> He gets too friendly, on the phone all the time, MSN, he uses it all up – they get a whole year's worth in two days. But because there are so many of them, he doesn't wear them out.

Some people have friends that they actually find a bit of a burden, and they don't mind it because they see it as a form of community service. It might be worth looking for someone like that to hang around with your child.

Talking with your child about why someone would be a good friend, what they might have to be good at and what the ingredients of a good friendship are could help your child to consider things they can do to make friends.

In Chapter 3, Learning, we consider the possibility of paying teenagers to do things with your child. You could stretch the idea a bit so they become a kind of paid friend. Some parents have found this idea quite difficult but anything you can do to get them into the habit of socializing is worth it.

You can sometimes influence your child's choice of peers, so comment positively about certain things. For example, 'I like that way Susie has of telling us about her favourite television programme' or 'Derek must be fun to be with'. Your approval can rub off on them.

Finally, peer groups are powerful. They can have more influence on your child than you. For example, if they prefer a particular fashion, band, phone, computer game or toy, you can bet your bottom dollar your child will want one too. Don't go overboard about it, but actually attending to these things at least a little bit can give them some serious street cred and help them to fit in.

If you try all of these ideas, and not a single one works, try again (after you've cried on one of your friend's shoulders; we're sure you'll have the odd one to draw on). That's the resilient approach, picking yourself up and trying again another time. Something might eventually stick, and children can change, often when you think it's least likely.

> When they moved class they had to name three kids they wanted to move with, and this best, and only, friend didn't name him. He dealt with it better than I did. He was quite positive he was going to meet other people. He had relied on this one child for years and if he wasn't around it was a major problem. I think he's turned the corner.

Conclusion

It's not hard to see that the idea of belonging is a universal human need and a central aspect of how we define who we are. And we hope we've shown in this chapter that there is a link between feeling like you belong and having had somebody to help you feel you belong. Of course our kids need more help than most, and that's partly why we've covered so much ground with this potion.

RT has relationships at the heart of its thinking. Children who have attachments that run deep and who possess a powerful sense of belonging do better than others, are more likely to make friends and to trust others. And even though it can be really frustrating and demoralizing when all your efforts seem fruitless, helping a child achieve a sense of belonging, wherever you can, is possibly the best thing you'll ever do for them.

When they're grown up, and can look back and say 'yes' to having even one of the following, rest assured that your efforts will not have been in vain.

- People around me I trusted and who loved me, no matter what.

- People who set limits for me so I knew when to stop before it was dangerous.

- People who showed me how to do things right by the way they did things.

- People who wanted me to learn to do things on my own.

- People who helped me when I didn't feel okay or was in trouble.

- People who helped me when I needed to learn.

- People who helped me when I was in danger or didn't feel safe.

Let's recap

Belonging – this potion helps a child make good relationships with family and friends.

- Find somewhere for the child to belong.

- Help child understand his/her place in the world.

- Tap into good influences.

- Keep relationships going.

- The more healthy relationships the better.

- Take what you can from any relationship where there is some hope.

- Get together people the child can count on.

- Belonging involves responsibilities and obligations too.

- Focus on good times and places.

- Make sense of where a child has come from.

- Predict a good experience of someone/something new.

- Help child make friends and mix with other children.

CHAPTER 3

LEARNING

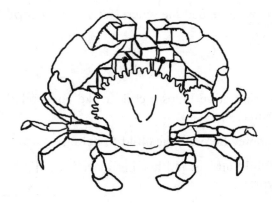

Introduction

This chapter gives us the opportunity to really focus on making learning work as well as it possibly can for our kids. It's an understatement to say that learning doesn't come as quickly and easily to our children as it does to others. As parents, we're often the ones who bear the brunt of teaching kids things that seem completely obvious to most people, day in day out. Living with children for whom mastering even the basics of life comes slowly, if at all, is tough. The really good news is that getting to grips with learning can make our own lives easier, as well as improve things for our children.

> It's taken me years to teach Jon to make a cup of tea. I've had to break it down into tiny steps, worry about me getting into trouble with social services if he ends up scalding himself, and put up with years of cold tea or finding a tea bag still lurking in the cup. But last Sunday he brought me up a cup of tea in bed (I did have to ask him) and it was vaguely drinkable. I felt so proud.

We know learning is essential to a child being able to function successfully in the world. It's not hard to see that it's fundamental to managing their lives resiliently. Making sense of their surroundings and the information they're given, adding this to what they already know and then working out how to apply it in the future is what learning is about.

Most of the resilience research on learning is specifically about schools. So from that we know that schooling matters hugely, it's a clear path to building resilience, and we certainly have a lot to say about schooling in this chapter. But as parents of course you'll know that children don't just learn how to do things, or how to be in the world, at school. They learn at home and in other situations out of school too, which is why this potion is not just about formal education, it's about informal learning too.

Making school life work, engaging mentors if need be, helping children to set goals in preparation for mapping out a career or life plan, developing life skills, helping them to organize themselves and highlighting achievements are all remedies included in the Learning potion. And, as you might expect from us by now, before we go on to explain more, it makes sense to reflect on your own thoughts and feelings about learning and schooling first.

Lots of people have negative associations with learning and, for some reason, 'not knowing' is often seen as a weakness that can make us feel anxious and uneasy. As you read more, notice how you feel about learning and the different remedies in this potion. Did you have tricky times at school and how do you feel about learning new things as an adult? Would you join a ballroom dancing class tomorrow when you reckon you've got two left feet, or is that a step (pardon the pun!) too far? However anxious it can make us feel, this potion encourages us to remember that learning is part of living and that just about every situation offers the possibility of finding out something new, however small. All children have the potential to learn, even if it's from the mistakes they make. It's a question of attitude and approach and how enthusiastic you are about expanding your child's horizons. So while you might be tired just reading this and prefer that you weren't so significant to your children's learning, the fact of the matter is you are!

Your experiences can hugely sway how you approach your child's learning. If you had a bad time at school, for example, it's possible that this could influence how you approach your child's schooling. (And if you had a brilliant time, it might be difficult for you to appreciate what it's like for a child who hates school.) The research on parents' attitudes to education is indisputable – if you value education, your children almost certainly will too. Essentially, your attitude to learning is the strongest influence on how successful a learner your child becomes. And did you know that, according to our calculations, children spend less than 20% of their waking hours, on average, at school?

Most of the time you're their teacher! So the more you know about how your child learns the better, and the more strategies you have to be patient and stick with it, the nicer life you'll have. Getting curious about how they learn can help you to know how to teach them well, although Angie sighs as we write this, saying 'it does wear a bit thin after a while'. But let's focus on the positive. Do you know how they learn best? Ever wondered why they like learning some things and not others?

Children are constantly learning through their senses, but often they have a preference. Some prefer to think and learn in pictures; they use their eyes to make sense of new information. Some prefer to use their ears and take in things mostly by what they hear. Others use their bodies and prefer to learn through actions and feelings. The point is, if we can tune into our children's preferences, chances are we can maximize their learning and help them to overcome some of the challenges they face. It helps us know how best to communicate with them.

See if you can work out your own preferred style. Angie's is definitely tied up with noise. She remembers making up songs to help her revise when she was at school. She tape-recorded herself singing French verbs and played it back constantly, much to the annoyance of everyone in the household. Sad, we know, but she didn't get out much in those days. So what about you? When you watch a film and someone asks you to describe it to them, do you explain what you've seen by recalling the pictures and images, the soundtrack, or the actions or feelings? Go on, try it. Maybe you use a mixture of all three? Now ask your child to describe their day at school – do they talk about what things looked like, sounded like, or what activities happened and how they felt about things?

Having this information about your child helps you tailor your approach, helping them learn most effectively. Children who prefer to learn with images and pictures respond well to us 'painting a picture' of things; books with illustrations or sketching things out visually, for example, help. Children who prefer to learn with sounds pay most attention to noises so they tend to remember what people have told them.

PLUGGING INTO YOUR CHILD'S LEARNING STYLE

Choose something small and specific that your child is trying to learn.

Now, if you were to help them with it, using just one of the three styles, how would you go about it?

- Using their eyes: think images, objects and pictures.
- Using their ears: think noises and sounds.
- Using their bodies: think actions, doing and feeling.

Educational toys with sounds and talking computer programs, for example, are likely to suit them. Be warned, though; because they're tuned into sounds they can get distracted easily so they might need quieter spaces for learning. And children who have a preference for thinking in actions and feelings are likely to learn best when they can do something while they're learning or have the chance to act it out somehow. Walking around while they're reading or doing maths problems while they're jumping about or on the swings are worth trying.

Of course, some children learn through all three styles and some use different styles for different things. While it really helps to know what your child's preferred way of learning is, it's also useful to expose them to the range of styles too – often referred to by professionals as the multi-sensory approach!

But whatever you do at home with your child, this is only part of the picture. Let's now go on to spend some time thinking about school.

Make school life work as well as possible

Research tells us that going to school regularly and doing well at school is one of the most helpful factors in supporting disadvantaged children to do better than expected. A positive school not only provides the place for academic achievement, it also offers a stable environment for learning other things, like getting along with adults as well as other children, finding out about established or accepted social ways of being, life skills and self-development. In effect it provides a structure within which to learn new things step by step, it offers access to people who can help and support you to do this, and it aims to educate in such a way that it builds children's self-esteem and 'know how', which they take with them into adult life. So it's worth doing all you can to get your child into a school environment where they are welcome (with all their quirky and challenging aspects) and, as far as possible, fit in.

But what does this mean for those of us whose children don't find school easy, straightforward or rewarding, who aren't welcome and don't fit in? Well, to pare it right down, we think it means two things. First, you keep on at it by committing to doing whatever you can to make school work for your child (as well as it can). Second, there's a big pay-off for you here, because if they're settled in school it will make your own life much easier. If you're not convinced, just talk to any parent who keeps getting phoned up by the school to come and discuss their child's behaviour.

Reflecting back on our previous section where we asked you to think about your own attitude to learning, it might be worth thinking a bit more about your attitude to school. Do you feel fine going into school meetings about your child, or does it make you feel like a powerless kid in a classroom again? Kim didn't enjoy school very much and she recalls it being quite a negative and discouraging experience on the whole. Thirty years later, even though she's been to hundreds of school meetings with parents to support them sorting things for their children, stepping into a school building still takes her back to those bad days. She says she always makes an effort to remind herself that her own experience is in the past so that she can leave it behind her and stay focused on being positive about negotiating with schools now.

DID YOU KNOW...

Children in the UK with special educational needs are nine times more likely to be permanently excluded from school than their peers without special educational needs. (DCSF 2008)

So what can we do to help our kids to get the best they can from school? Well, we've already mentioned that it matters to work out your child's preferred learning style; however, understanding their ability level, and making sure they're in a school that can realistically support this, probably matters even more.

And one of the things that lots of parents have told us helps is asking professionals to provide them with an age-equivalent score for their child's different abilities. It's meant they've been able to pitch their approach at home in a way that best fits with wherever their child is at.

> When she asked me how old I thought she was in her head, and I said about six, even though it's her thirteenth birthday next week, I suddenly thought what I was expecting of her was too hard.

> Once I remembered that emotionally I was dealing with a toddler, I knew what to do to help him change so he didn't upset so many of the other children in his class.

Children's ability to communicate and understand what's being said, concentrate and pay attention, use a pencil or pick up small objects, copy from a book, remember things, or run, skip and catch a ball can vary widely. It's likely that your child won't fit tidily with the developmental chart we included in the introduction because they're not progressing at the same rate across all of these areas at the same time. Children with complex needs usually don't. They might be doing really well in one area and not another or they might be making progress with different things at different speeds. Often the usual milestones that signal a shift can be less obvious as a result of their disability or special educational need. Or sometimes we adults have low expectations of what they are capable of so we don't notice the subtle changes. Keeping up with where they are isn't easy if progress is hard to detect.

Having said that, checking out your child's abilities is quite important because it's information that can help you work with them at the right level. Regular contact with your child's school probably needs to be the norm for you, because in order to assess what your child is capable of in different areas, you need to talk to their teachers or other professionals who might be supporting them at school. And you need to constantly review it. Herein lies the rub. Of all the issues parents have raised with us over the years, dealing with schools and education authorities is the thorniest. Knowing the right questions to ask, getting the information you need, making sense of professional reports and staying engaged with the whole education system and process for children with special educational needs is quite simply hard work. And the bottom line is we want our children to be happy and want to go to school. Enlist others in the task.

> It's great to see Jessica standing outside the door in her uniform smiling and waving at the school minibus before it's even arrived. Two years ago, I never thought she could ever be so happy about going off to school. And what's more, as a result my own life has been transformed.

In our experience, getting regular feedback from your child's school and exchanging useful information means you have to establish a constructive way of working with them, as partners. You might find the hints about school meetings of some use.

School meetings

BEFOREHAND

Meetings often go better when you prepare. It helps you to feel more at ease. Decide what you want to get out of the meeting and make a note of it to look at during the meeting if you get sidetracked.

Make a list of questions and points you want to raise and take it with you, because it's not so easy to think on the spot – well, not if you're our age anyway.

Think about asking someone to go with you. They don't have to do anything necessarily, but they can offer emotional support and prompt you if you forget what you want to say.

Check out how you're feeling about approaching the school and, if you're anxious, upset or angry, think about why, and try some of the ideas in the Coping chapter, to calm yourself down.

AT THE MEETING

Ask questions and keep asking until whatever is unclear is explained in a way that makes sense to you.

Before you finish the meeting, summarize what you think has been said and what people are agreeing to do next.

Make an appointment to meet up again to review things if necessary. It's good to make this appointment then and there, so remember your diary or take your calendar along, to save you ringing around later. You can always cancel the appointment if you find you don't need it later on.

AFTER THE MEETING

Jot down what was agreed because you might forget the detail in a few months' time. It helps to keep a record of all that's gone on. Apart from reminding you of the hard work you're putting in, if things get problematic and people haven't done what they said they would, you've got something to refer back to.

Message for professionals

Anything you can do to help parents manage the heavy schedule of meetings they have will be appreciated. One of the common frustrations mentioned by parents time and time again is that they have to repeat their stories and say the same things over and over – they'd welcome a bit of co-ordination.

Having said all that, we doubt you can ensure that school is trouble free – life just doesn't happen like that very often for children with complex needs (and if it does, enjoy it while it lasts!).

If you do have a difficult meeting coming up, anything you can do for yourself to get into a positive state beforehand, the better. For example, think of being in your favourite place in the world and imagine being there, before you go.

It's equally important for children to be in a positive learning state when they are at school so you can use this same technique with them. And if you are having a battle, aim to hide your negative feelings from your child because they will pick up that something is wrong and this will hinder their learning – positive feelings speed it up.

For those children who get anxious about going, one of the quickest ways to shift their thinking is to ask them what it's like to be happy, or excited or glad (choose some feeling they like to be in). It works because they can only answer your question if they think and feel the emotion you've asked them to call to mind.

> When she says she doesn't want to go to school, which is most mornings of late, I ask her to look up at the sky and imagine she's on the swings in the park. She usually gets a smile on her face and we set off.

Asking children to get a picture of themselves doing a fun activity or, even better, having a really fun time in class learning, or concentrating well or learning easily, can raise their confidence about learning and it can set their focus for the day. Another tack is to tell children firmly that the law says they have to go to school, and that both you and they will be in trouble if they don't. If these simple strategies don't work, chances are that something more serious is going on. In this case, you'll probably need to enlist other people to help you get to the bottom of the problem. Positive partnerships between parents and school that focus on getting a child's educational needs met are fundamental to getting school right. We carry on thinking about who else can help in the next section.

Engage mentors for children

We know from research that children do better in school if they have one, or a few, trusted individuals to whom they can turn when things get tricky, and who act as role models for their learning. Various studies show that having a special adult in their life can make a world of difference to a child feeling worthwhile – and if they feel worthwhile, they're likely to learn better. This idea works outside of school too, and increasingly it applies to peer relationships, with peer support being a valuable way of helping troubled kids.

Mentors – adult or peer – are a good vehicle for this. They are volunteers or paid individuals who get to know specific children. Some schools, for example, have mentoring schemes that involve older pupils looking after younger ones. Mentors support children's development and learning in a range of situations; spend time getting to know them and gain their trust.

So mentors are people who are confident to work with children with complex needs, accepting them warts and all, and becoming a listening ear, supporting them emotionally and practically to get what they need in life. This can be especially helpful for our children because mentors can tailor their style to individual need. It's a made to measure approach, because as we know, when it comes to children with special needs, one size doesn't fit all.

If your child needs someone to assist them to get to school and support them through the day it might be worth exploring mentoring. Find out first if your child already has a learning mentor in school – they may do and you may not know about it, so it's worth asking. If they haven't got one at the moment, find out if your child's school has a scheme, and ask for them to be considered for it. If you don't ask, you won't get.

Outside school, there are community and voluntary organizations that organize mentorship schemes for children with complex needs, and the council sometimes sets them up too. Of course, you can be quite inventive about enlisting people to mentor your child. Members of your wider family are obvious ports of call – they might have hobbies they would be willing to share with your child, or they might take them on day trips, or help them with homework, etc. Failing that (or as additional support, the more the merrier perhaps, because, let's face it, some people have quite a low tolerance threshold) there might be someone who lives nearby and could help with reading or homework – and can often do it better than us because they don't have the same relationship with your child. Look for someone in the neighbourhood who could act as a homework mentor – a first-year university student might be interested.

But don't just think about adults – what about older children who can act as mentors? As we said earlier, the value of this is becoming increasingly recognized. Maybe someone who is part of a local club and is planning a teaching career could help you out:

He sees him twice a week, once when they are in the group and once on his own to practise. He is slowly improving.

So think creatively. If your child can't go out alone, and doesn't have friends to go with, maybe you know a teenager who would be interested in taking on a mentoring role. We feel quite strongly that, to make it happen, realistically you'll have to pay the teenager or find something else to give them if you're completely broke. Or you might be lucky to find someone who does it for the joy of working with children with complex needs, or for something positive on their CV if they plan to go into teaching for example.

> It's great that I've employed 16-year-old Rachel to go to the park with Dotty twice a week. Dotty's 16 too, but doesn't have any friends of her own, so she loves seeing Rachel and going out with someone her own age who she can look up to, and who keeps her safe. Once I explained to Rachel that Dotty has learning difficulties and needed a mentor, she was really thrilled to be given the job. I make sure I tell her how grateful I am that she can support Dotty so well, and my reference came in very handy when she applied for university.

If these ideas don't work, try getting a mentor more subtly. Which of your friends' older children would you like your child to model themselves on? Once you've identified them, create times when both families get together and overlap – children are much less conscious of age differences in family situations than they are in school, giving a better chance that they'll mix well together.

When it works well, mentoring really can be an excellent experience for both parties. Mentors enjoy being asked for their advice and your child might enjoy sharing ideas and concerns with someone older, who may or may not be an adult, but crucially is not you.

Setting goals: mapping out a career or life plan

> You've got to be joking – she's only three years old!

Indeed, you're probably thinking your child is too young to be considering a life plan or a career just yet. But in our experience, when it comes to learning, we could all benefit from thinking ahead more often than we usually do. Research doesn't yet tell us if certain ambitions mean that kids will do better in the long run. But it does suggest something about children who have a strong sense of purpose and who think about how they would like their futures to be. They behave in resilient ways in the here and now.

> To be quite honest I used to dread thinking about the future because there was lots of unanswered stuff and stuff I didn't know, it

just freaked me out. But when I faced it, and spoke to some other parents, it really helped.

So as hard as it may seem to contemplate the future for those of us bringing up and caring for children with complex needs, it's a good thing to do. Thinking ahead and imagining where you'd like your child to be in three months or a year or two (and we don't mean dreaming they are totally independent of you here!) can help us make decisions about what gets learned now and what gets dropped or left for another time. This remedy is all about widening horizons. Having a mindset with a view to the future can set children up for eventually mapping out a meaningful adult life. Hard to imagine just yet, we know.

We appreciate you might be using all your resources to manage the present, but dipping your toe into tomorrow can set up a whole series of chain reactions that promote resilience. Kim recalls going to a school meeting with a parent of an 11-year-old to discuss their progress and noticing how refreshing it was when the head teacher wanted to know from each of the people at the meeting where they hoped this child would be in five years' time. She said it really focused the discussion and helped all the adults in the room, including the teachers, speech and language therapist and the parent, to work backwards.

It's obvious that you'll be making all the important decisions for your children while they're young. But this remedy shows you can do things now that can help them practise for when they're older. Ask children for their thoughts and views. Even if it's hard to be sure what they mean or you don't know if they can think through what's best, one of the most important things we can give them is the belief that they and their views matter. You could experiment by building in opportunities for your child to get involved in making everyday choices. It's harder to make important decisions if you haven't had lots of practice-making smaller ones. However, too much choice can be overwhelming so agree what's practical and keep the number of alternatives to two or three. You could model decision-making as a family so that everyone has a chance to say what they think. It's okay to have different ideas and change your mind after listening to other views, and everyone agrees to go with the majority decision or the adult's final word, just in case.

Setting goals is a good way to introduce the idea of working towards some desired end, no matter how young a child. Children who can set goals and work towards reaching them are more likely to be successful in later life. So stringing together a series of steps over time can slowly help a child to realize longer-term ambitions. Of course, things can get a bit trickier when you have a child with mad ideas about what they can do. What you're aiming for with this remedy is to strengthen your child's capacity to make realistic plans and carry them out.

In a moment's idleness with your child (of course you've got nothing better to do!), you could try brainstorming a few ideas about where they want to be in, say, two weeks', six weeks' or twelve weeks' time. Work up to five years if you're really looking to fill some time! Then, if your enthusiasm hasn't waned, think about the steps needed to achieve these goals, writing or drawing them onto small slips of paper (you just happen to have handily lying around), to remind you and your child to go back to them later.

Up for taking this idea further? Draw a time line on a large piece of paper with the intervals of time that seem to fit whatever it is you are aiming to achieve.

TARGET SETTING

Here is an example of a time line:

[*Now*…in 2 weeks' time…in 6 weeks' time…in 12 weeks' time, etc.…*Future goal*]

Now ask your child to paste the slips of paper in the appropriate spaces. Voila. They should now have a visual plan for how they are going to achieve their final target that they can stick up on the wall to remind them every day of the steps they are taking to reaching it, doubling up as a valuable piece of art work.

For most of us, succeeding at anything is easier if we have an end in mind. Ask your child what they think it might feel like when they can cook their own meals, spell their own name and address, travel to school or use a bus alone.

If they've thought about what it will be like in the end, they're more likely to keep going until they can do it. Having a visual image can prompt them to stay on track. Knowing how to do a cartwheel is easier to put into practice if you have a mental picture of what someone doing a cartwheel looks like. But you have to keep the image in the forefront of your mind. We've tried to imagine ourselves as perfect parents, but it's too ridiculous to stay focused on!

Promoting learning and thinking ahead is an investment for the future – you can make a big difference to your children's chances in life. But how do you motivate children to stick at things? Here are a few ideas we've collected from colleagues and parents:

Keeping at it

- Pick your time – the timing might not be right so avoid flogging a dead horse.

- Set positive goals – 'remember your homework' is better than 'don't forget your homework'.

- Practise setting goals as part of your household routine – so everyone knows that clearing the kitchen up has to happen before watching a special TV programme, for example.

- Encourage them to try again if they fail – it's okay to make mistakes, we learn from them.

- Be a role model yourself by talking about how you're going to get a task done, and congratulating yourself when you completed it in time.

Develop life skills

If you think about it, just about everything we do involves a strategy, whether we know it or not – brushing our teeth, finding a pen, getting to work. But if someone was to ask us how we do any of these things, we'd probably struggle to explain – 'I don't know, I just do it.'

This remedy is about teaching children the necessary skills for living – which for many children with complex needs don't come so naturally and need to be broken down into stages. They're skills that can be hard to teach, because sometimes we don't even realize they are skills and if we can do them easily anyway we're not on the whole very aware of what's involved.

The idea of life skills can be quite difficult for children to understand, but asking them will give you an idea of what they're thinking, and where their aspirations might lie.

Angie asked her 13-year-old daughter with complex needs what she thought people needed to get by in life, and she said: put money in a charity box, be good at hard work, do some essays, play musical instruments, do some more cleaning, do a big job and save up to buy things. Her 15-year-old son, also with complex needs, said: love, care, have people who will help you, be independent. Kim asked her typically developing 17-year-old daughter the same thing. She said: cycling, swimming, writing, speaking, eating, playing with friends, listening, working with people.

However you or your children define life skills, without even realizing it you'll be incorporating teaching these sort of things into your daily interactions with your children already. Or not? We're assuming that there are likely to be things your child is not getting the hang of so easily. Or that you've grown so accustomed to their dependent way that you don't realize that they still can't tie their shoe laces or go to the toilet on their own, because you've come to accept that's just how they are.

Kim remembers a mother telling her that her son still couldn't manage weeing standing up and, when she asked about this a bit more, it was clear that he'd never seen his dad doing this at home as it wasn't the norm in the family to be open about toileting.

Being successful at teaching life skills probably relies on us being willing and able to break these things down into small parts, so we can teach them to our children – and you might have to enlist the help of others occasionally! Developing life skills is about relating learning to real life and children need your help to do this.

One of the best ways to help children to learn life skills is to start with something they already know and attach new information to it in some way. If your kids have learnt how to make a mean cheese sandwich, don't stop there. Expand on this to include ham and cucumber. The greatest teachers (you of course!) can relate new pieces of information to something that's already familiar to your child. Finding ways to make the connections really helps.

When you start thinking about how you might teach your child life skills think about doing it in the most appropriate environment in the best state of mind. Not much point teaching a child to dress themselves if you're exasperated and already late for school. It goes without saying, doesn't it, that making things fun, enjoyable and a little challenging makes for good learning conditions.

Children won't learn much if they're bored either. Think about the last time you chose to learn something new – what was it that got you started? Were you just interested in the subject, enthused by someone, fancied the instructor? Or maybe it was because it was relevant to your life, you could see the positives or you thought it would be fun. Children need to be motivated to learn so it might help if you can hook into whatever's driving them to make the effort. Or more to the point, if school is requiring them to learn something that they seem totally disinterested in, what can you do to spur them on?

> I make sure they know we all have to do things we don't like – for really good reasons. I say to them, 'Do you really think I like going to the supermarket to get the shopping?' They understand it when it's to do with food!

KEEPING AT IT!

Think of something specific that you managed to learn successfully, but at the time you didn't want to learn it. Choose something that you're now glad you learned. Write it down here.

Now, write down a few words about what kept you at it; what kept you trying to learn it? Even when you felt really unmotivated or just didn't want to do it, what helped you to carry on with it?

If you find it helpful, why not try this exercise with your child?

We don't usually gather new ideas and skills overnight. It takes a bit of patience, time and effort. Learning new things usually means keeping at it and persevering.

As we discuss in the problem-solving remedy in the next chapter (Coping) real learning usually happens when children are slightly out of their comfort zone. You don't want to raise the bar so high that they give up, but nor do you want to make things so easy that they lose interest because there's no challenge involved. Children learn best from slightly difficult tasks that they have to work at. Make things too easy and they're unlikely to learn to persevere and, if your child doesn't learn to stick at things and gives up too easily, they'll do less well in life.

When embarking on teaching the next life skill, focus clearly on what you want them to achieve and have an end in mind. Then practise, which usually means having a go, correcting and fiddling with things until it's right and then doing it again. And if this doesn't work, consider alternative solutions because there's usually more than one way to crack a nut.

Often, if children want something they'll try harder to get it or they'll change something they're doing to improve their odds. The 'wanting' can be a great motivator. Most children are very self-interested – learning to think of others comes later, fingers crossed.

You can increase a child's motivation by simply being enthusiastic and interested; it can be contagious. And for those of us who have less well-motivated children, there's nothing stopping us from introducing a few incentives ourselves. Rewards and treats can play a big part in children's lives.

We really do appreciate that all of this is clearly easier said than done with many of the children we know and love. Sometimes, despite all your hard work, they might not be getting it at all. There's an obvious tension between expecting lots and accepting our kids' limitations. You might think that low expectations might protect them from not achieving things. However, the opposite is often true.

Help a child to organize themselves

We focused on toileting because he didn't have a clue, so how was he going to manage at school? So we put pictures on the bathroom wall to remind him of the different parts to it – shut the door, pull your trousers down, use the paper, flush, wash your hands, use soap, dry your hands. But we didn't do it all at once, we just concentrated on one part at a time and added more pictures each time he got the hang of the earlier stage.

As we sit trying to think of some tips for this section, we come out with a long list of ideas that we see in some of the parenting manuals, and Angie laughs that she struggles to put them into practice herself. And yet, when she does, family life runs more smoothly and life works much better for her children.

Many of these following ideas will seem quite obvious. But it's worth checking out if you really are doing them.

Getting organized

- Get organized yourself – decide what you really need, get rid of the rest and order what's left.

- Agree places to store things. It avoids wasting time hunting for them, and having a 'home' for things like the car keys, scissors and glue all helps create a less hectic atmosphere in the home.

- Sort out the kids' clothes and lunch boxes the night before so you're not dashing around in the morning. Make sure they have everything they need for school.

- If your life is really chaotic you might need help to organize a routine at home – regular mealtimes for the whole family and slots for television, homework and playtime.

- Spend some time devising a simple set of chores that are carried out at regular times – and build in some rewards if necessary. A regular plan for everyday jobs like tidying up, dusting the surfaces, washing the dishes after mealtimes, weeding, cleaning the car and walking the dog, is likely to work best.

- Keep it simple and specific. Children with complex needs often need things to be very concrete and it can help to use more than words to get your message across.

- Demonstrate the task and show them what you mean rather than just talking about it.

- Break down jobs into smaller steps. For example, if your child's task is to set the table, first ask her to get the right number of forks. Then have her put one at each family member's place at the table. Do the same with the knives, going one at a time. Praise your child when she manages it.

- And you can write things down or use pictures, objects or examples to help them remember what the job involves.

It can be important to know how your child organizes their thinking. Apparently laughing can help you remember things. Kim's oldest daughter has mild dyspraxia – she always drops things, routinely walks into doorframes and struggles to get organized. Kim says she guessed there might be a problem when she ended up with the family-sized bowl of trifle in her lap for the third time! When she asked her how she copes with being naturally disorganized, she said she writes loads of lists and has learnt to prioritize keeping her room tidy.

> If my room gets in a mess it upsets everything – I can't find a thing and it makes me panic and then the rest of my life gets in a mess. There's no half measures – it can't be a little bit cluttered, it's got to be really sorted otherwise everything comes unstuck.

Highlight achievements

In Chapter 5, Core Self, we mention the value of fostering a child's talents and in Chapter 4, Coping, we discuss the importance of fostering their interests. And now we've included highlighting achievements in this Learning chapter. Get the feeling we're trying to promote something? Well, we all want our children to feel a touch of success in some way.

All these remedies link well together and build resilience. The difference with highlighting achievements is that it's about really shouting out about anything they do remotely well, playing to their strengths. Noticing their successes matters because otherwise it's easy for our kids – and us too sometimes – to think they're no good at anything.

> My six-year-old eventually learnt to say 'milk' in a way that other people understood her. You'd think she'd managed to swim the Channel and back if you saw how much we praised her, ringing up her granny and telling her; we were all so pleased we nearly put an advert in the local paper, and she was thrilled with herself.

In Britain especially we're quite good at playing down any compliments, so it might be quite a challenge for some of us to get into the habit of routine praise. You're looking to build positive comments about the little everyday successes into your daily conversations with kids. And we mean praising successes of all sorts, not just academic ones.

When your child does something well, or improves on their last effort, get into the habit of noticing and commenting on it. You know, using that tried and tested phrase 'well done', or being more specific is even better: 'You've put loads of effort into that, brilliant.'

It's important for children to know what they do well so that they can do it more often or improve on it.

There's a link between how you and they think about their chances of succeeding at learning. Your child's assumption about their ability to learn is likely to mirror yours so it helps if they hear you praising them to your friends or telling the family how well they've done at school or with learning to ride a bike or bath themselves, for example.

> Someone bought me one of those baby books when she was born, where you paste in photos and record the date when they start walking and talking. I felt a bit miserable at the time but I've adapted it and listed all the things she can do, even though most of them seem small to other people. Now she adds things to it as well.

Asking your children how they like to be praised is worthwhile, as you wouldn't want to embarrass them, especially in public, now would you? And understanding from their point of view what they think they are good at can provide them with practice for saying positive things about themselves out loud. The very act of giving words and voice to their achievements soaks in under the skin a little faster and they begin to believe they are really good at things.

And when there are failures – of which there are likely to be many – you could try helping them to see that mistakes are part of learning too. Modelling this is a really useful way to make the idea of mistakes okay in your family life.

> Whenever I cook something and it's a disaster – which is a bit more often than I like to admit – we have this ritual of everyone suggesting ways to make it better; then we have to agree one thing that was good about the meal – usually it's just that it was hot, or there was enough of it!

Conclusion

Resilience is strongly linked with academic achievement and educational success. The resilience research base points time and time again to the value of doing well at school – it's as powerful as 'belonging' if you want to help a child to do better than expected.

But we've used the idea of learning in its broadest sense in this potion because we think it deepens the possibilities of trying to change things for the better. School is fundamentally important, and getting it right can massively improve your child's life and yours too. But this chapter also addresses the significance of helping children to develop their life skills, notice their achievements, organize themselves, set goals and map out life plans and use mentors to good advantage more generally in life.

It goes without saying that you'll probably have to call on the noble truth of commitment to get anywhere with the learning potion – there's real effort required, for us and for our children, to learn new ways of thinking and doing. And while we're on the subject of noble truths, perhaps we should have included a fifth when it comes to helping children with complex needs to learn – patience (we struggle here ourselves!).

But, with a bit of good humour, creativity and good timing when it seems like it's impossible to influence any shifts, and things can't get much worse, change happens. We've seen it time and time again.

And let's not forget the excitement of learning. It broadens horizons and you can model adventure, making it safe for them to have a go too.

When was the last time you tried something adventurous, or even something a little bit new? Exactly – we can get so entangled with helping our children to learn that we forget to try new things out ourselves. Why not give it a go yourself now?

Let's recap

Learning – this not only includes school education, but also helping with their life skills, talents and interests.

- Make school life work as well as possible.

- Engage mentors for children.

- Map out career/life plan.

- Develop life skills.

- Help the child to organize her/himself.

- Highlight achievements.

CHAPTER 4

COPING

Introduction

It's not uncommon, is it, to hear people chatting (or moaning!) about how they're busy coping with life and managing difficult times. And the parents who've helped with this book had no trouble understanding the Coping potion. But when we really discussed it with them in detail, they hadn't actually unpacked coping as an idea. When they did, they found it very helpful, and noticed they were coping experts and that they could learn from each other. So in this chapter we're going to spell out, first, something about what coping means and, second, actual ways of doing it in practice.

Having read lots about coping, we think the word describes the efforts we make to master, tolerate or minimize a whole load of demands that stress us out. And while these demands can be put on us by society (sometimes unfairly), some of us create more problems for ourselves just by the way we are. Ouch, sound familiar? Coping might mean we actually have to do some things differently in the world, or change the way we think or feel about things.

Many children pick up how to cope fairly easily as they go through life – and we bet you know what the next sentence is going to say. That's right, for our children, learning to cope takes extra effort! We often think what an irony it is that the very children who need coping skills the most are actually the least likely to pick them up without loads of help.

Our Coping potion is about building up a particular set of skills in children to help them get by in everyday life. And like Basics, it's a very practical, and some might say almost superficial, RT potion that favours building children's outer skills rather than focusing on their deeper inner thoughts. But of course you can't really separate the two so tidily. All the RT potions are interconnected so making changes on the outside will have a knock-on effect and change the inside anyway. Like having a shower and putting clean clothes on, you end up feeling fresher within!

There are times for all of us when life can be pretty unbearable and when we find ourselves in situations that we can't control. The truth is, the stresses of living are less bothersome if you can cope with them. But children can learn how to deal with difficulties resiliently. While we do understand that there are many things that children should never be expected to cope with, the fact is that sometimes they just have to, and helping them cope is the best way forward. RT's coping skills range from learning to 'fake it until you make it' right through to developing the talent to sit with horrible feelings, in the knowledge that 'this time will pass'. In this chapter, we illustrate ways of learning some of these skills.

But first off, we have to find out whether children believe they have any control over what they do and what happens to them. What's your child's current locus of control? Pardon? Well, we could have used different language at this point, but we thought you might appreciate having a giggle at the jargon. This is the way researchers and some professionals refer to how children see themselves in relation to:

1. how well they can take charge of their own actions and feelings (self-efficacy)

2. how much they think they can direct their own lives (self-regulation).

Individuals who have a strong internal locus of control tend to think they're responsible for their own destiny and can make things happen in their lives. Whereas individuals with a strong external locus of control tend to think of themselves as victims, on the receiving end of what others do and less able to influence the things that happen in their lives. If you want to develop a resilient mindset, having a sense that you can influence your life is a step in the right direction.

Doing this exercise with your child might better illustrate what we mean. It can be really helpful to find out how in control your children feel about their lives, because it can give you some pointers for what has to happen next. And even if they're too young, or their particular needs mean they wouldn't be able to understand this quiz properly, it might give you some ideas of where you're trying to get to with them.

WHO MAKES THINGS HAPPEN?

Ask your child to answer these questions with a yes or no:

1. When bad things happen to you is it usually someone else's fault?

2. When you get good marks at school is it just that you've been lucky?

3. When a friend is angry with you, is it usually your fault or theirs?

4. When someone's cross with you, can you make them your friend again?

5. When you get into an argument or fight is it usually the other person's fault?

6. Are you surprised when someone tells you you've done well?

7. Do you feel you've done well if you beat up a whole load of people?

8. Are you proud of yourself if you manage to steal something without getting caught?

9. Do you think if you work harder, you'll get better marks?

So how did they do? If they said 'yes' a lot, it's likely they've got quite a strong internal locus of control. But take another look at their answers to 7 and 8. If they answered yes to these, you might be worried, or you might be impressed that they were recognizing some of the less desirable aspects of their own personality! The point here is that this simplistic quiz can't capture all the subtlety of communication between you and your child. And kids recognizing things in this little quiz and actually behaving that way in the real world might not match. So take the quiz with a pinch of salt, but if you write down their answers now and do it again in a few months after you've tried some of the ideas in this chapter, you may find their mindset has changed, let's hope for the better!

One further point of caution. Having an overly strong internal locus of control is not always a good thing. Hitler no doubt had one! And some children have an unrealistic sense of their own power, or their ability to understand any of these ideas may be lacking. But overall it is a useful way of thinking, if you use your common sense with it. Children who do have an idea that they have some control over what happens to them in life are going to do a better job of managing their life resiliently.

If you find that your child has a very weak locus of control, don't despair. Use the noble truth of accepting. It's a chance to be creative and discover what resilient moves you can make to get them to a better place. Easier said than done, we know, but we think it's worth giving it a try. And by the way, doing this quiz with your child might have made you wonder whether you have a strong locus of control yourself. On a scale of 1–10, how much control do you feel you have to direct your life?

CAN I DIRECT MY LIFE?

Not at all   Lots

0. 10

So, what would you have to do to move yourself up the scale towards 10?

When it comes to your children, you might find yourself having to go overboard to help them notice when they do cope so that they eventually get the hang of their own power and influence. And you might have to teach them to pretend sometimes – fake it until they make it. Most of us will have been in situations where we've felt stupid, haven't understood what was being said or felt attacked. Acting in the opposite way, 'as if' we weren't stupid, that we were grasping what was being said or didn't feel threatened, can help us cope. In much the same way as we mention in Chapter 5, Core Self, when children are managing such deep lows that they want to stay in bed all day, acting 'as if' they're feeling buoyant by getting up and doing something productive when they don't want to can help them cope with their feelings of depression.

> It's almost as though the pretending gets under your skin and lodges there so that you end up really believing and knowing you can cope.

And it can be equally powerful to help children to appreciate that while bad things happen to everyone, they don't stay that way forever – everything is changing all the time.

Children learn coping skills when things are going badly. They can't learn them when things are going well. So, if coping is a question of how you handle what's thrown at you, what are the skills worth learning?

Understand boundaries and keep within them

We all act on our impulses, urges and whims sometimes. Kim asks embarrassing questions that English people find offensive and regrets it later and Angie lets in every waif and stray when she hasn't got the energy to look after them all.

By boundaries, we mean setting and keeping within limits. They might be limits we set ourselves or that others set us like laws and social conventions. Sounds simple enough doesn't it, but anyone with a child with complex needs will know it's often not so straightforward. Working out what the right limits are, getting children to stick to them or when to let up a bit can be incredibly difficult. Research gives us a few pointers here. Parents who get it most right seem to be fairly strict, but also very nice with it. Kids with complex needs often do well in families that are a bit like a benevolent boot camp. Lots of rules that they know they have to keep, and parents that take a real interest in what they are doing, where they are, and manage to convey all this without sounding like nasty old bags. Hmmm, not easy, we know, but persevering with keeping tabs on your kids and with helping them stick to boundaries, even if it all seems to fall completely on deaf ears, appears to work in their best interests in the long run.

Understanding boundaries and keeping within them is often confusing for children. For some it can mean keeping to rules and a rigid way of operating that they don't like while for others it can mean having expectations laid out clearly that are hard to remember or to stay focused on. And for those children who have difficulty with their anger or who maybe have a biological tendency to be impulsive, it can be particularly challenging. Practising self-restraint and self-regulation is going to take some serious effort. And of course it's not easy for you either.

> When he kicks off, there's something that goes on for me emotionally, so I get in a state, then there's the practical coping strategy dealing with the behaviour, then there's the coping with his emotions. It's hard to do all that at once and get on the outside looking in.

We can't tell you that trying this way or that will necessarily work for your particular situation. But we do know that there are a few things about setting boundaries that will help to build resilience, and we've organized them into four points.

Point 1: Setting boundaries is a safety thing

Setting firm boundaries can help children to feel safe so, even when you think they might not be working, hang in there and keep going. We know from research that children's resilience is linked with firm, persistent and caring supervision from their parents or carers. Setting limits that provide practical protection and warn children off dangerous situations is obvious enough – like banning younger ones from playing with matches or boiling a hot kettle. But things get a little more complicated when we're insisting children protect themselves from more subtle risks like not befriending strangers or when we're trying to establish boundaries for bad behaviour.

There are loads of books written about managing children's behaviour positively, so we don't intend to repeat the same here or go into too much detail – skip to the end of the book for a few ideas of other things to read if you want more detail and further information. But if you feel like you've lost the plot and your child's behaviour is taking over, we suggest you grit your teeth and get it sorted as early as possible. Children need routine and structure to feel safe and they need clear boundaries so they know where they stand. And while you want to reward them when they do well they also need to understand the consequences when they don't do so well, so they can learn from their mistakes – even if it's ever so slowly.

In our experience you need to decide what the limits will be before you can sort out how to teach children to operate within them. And if their behaviour's all over the place and you're having trouble seeing the wood from the trees, sometimes listing the problems, clustering them into themes and then into priority order can help you work out where to begin. Then from here you can begin to think about how you'd ideally like your child to behave, checking you're being realistic about what you want, of course. Cross off any battles you can afford not to bother fighting. You might find you need to compromise a little or adjust your expectations, because they may not be functioning at the same level as their chronological age. But once you've done this, decide what to tackle first. Trying to do it all at once will almost certainly end in tears. Break it down for your sake and theirs!

> Learning to say no was much harder than I expected, and I felt really upset about it. I think I was trying to compensate for things. I knew he wasn't feeling well and it was tough for him at school, so giving into him was my way of trying to make his days nicer. But I made a rod for my own back and it didn't do him any favours either.

Don't assume your children can read your mind, although they are often very good at picking up on your mood, which can come in handy when trying to convey your authority! You need to communicate what your limits are as clearly and precisely as you can and this might mean not just telling them what you expect, but showing them you mean business. Using the right tone of voice, being consistent, not giving in and standing firm are all ways of making your actions speak louder than words.

> I got so fed up shouting and nagging him, I almost gave up. I suppose I hit rock bottom so I had nowhere else to go. I could go on shouting or I could practise being calm, even if it was just surface stuff. I sort of let him know I was boss, but I asked nicely and then, if he ignored me, I got more firm and a bit louder. He got the message eventually, especially when his pocket money got docked.

Ignoring tantrums, praising good behaviour, holding back rewards or withdrawing privileges are recommended time and time again by the behaviour experts. And introducing the idea of time out is another useful tip.

> It wasn't easy putting her in the hallway, away from us all. But by about the tenth time, I think she realized it was boring being on her own. So what started out as five minutes' time out reduced down to just the threat of it!

But probably the most important thing about boundaries is being consistent and realistic. Most of us have probably threatened our kids with something completely ridiculous, like: 'If you don't tidy your bedroom I'll make you wash my feet!' If you're in that exhausted group of parents, who can make a bit of an effort on a good day but don't really believe that setting limits is going to make much difference, it's probably best not to even try. Come back to it when you've recharged your batteries because holding the boundaries can take quite a bit of sweat and toil at first. But the sooner you can muster the strength the better.

Point 2: Developing the idea of a bottom line

This is a really helpful idea to keep hold of with children struggling with boundaries. While this can be about safety too, children's self-esteem and sense of worth increases when they know that others care enough about them to set boundaries. So next time you're feeling a bit harsh, trust your judgement and hold the line.

> Sometimes I make an active decision to say 'Yes, you can'. That to me is coping. I have weighed up the pros and cons and decided okay we'll do that for 20 minutes. But sometimes it's not so thought out and I just react and I think, damn, he's done it again!

Point 3: Asking your child what they might like to improve themselves

No doubt you'll already have a good idea of what boundary they have trouble sticking to, but if you can get their co-operation, you're onto a winner.

In our experience, it's not very helpful being dogmatic. Sometimes we can only see things through our own frazzled, hectic and subjective eyes. You might think they need to kiss you goodbye before they run off into the school playground, but they might think it's more important to find someone to hang out with as quickly as possible. And remember, children's ability to manage restrictions changes over time. We wouldn't want to rule out their making a cup of tea or lighting a match as they get older, so what was not okay in the past may be acceptable now and vice versa. Reviewing boundaries is a great way to involve them in experimenting with setting and sticking to limits.

For children who don't provide ready answers to questions, ask them for their 'best guess' or tell them what your 'best hunch' is if they're struggling, as they'll soon let you know if you're way off the mark. And giving attention to just one thing for a specific period of time or a clear number of occasions can concentrate a child's attention.

> Cheng said he wanted to stay out playing in the park later. So I said we could try it as long as he was in by 6 p.m. without fail. We agreed to do it for a week and then see how it went. Of course he wasn't back by 6 – he can't read the time! We got round that one by working out how to use the alarm on his watch.

Point 4: Fitting in

Personally we both love free spirits, but we recognize that kids like ours thrive better if they can fit in wherever possible. Living within commonly held social rules helps children to get on in the world but they need to know what these rules are before they can learn to keep within them. We don't mean universal morals here (more of that in Chapter 5, Core Self), but those generally accepted social norms that we take for granted like saying hello when you meet someone, queuing at the checkout, not dropping litter or thanking people when they help you out. Crossing these basic socially accepted boundaries will almost always get children into trouble.

The following exercise might be a useful starting point to talk about boundaries with your child. Ask them to colour any of the boxes they think are about behaving well and being good. And before you ask them, you could ask yourself which of the list you think they already understand.

> We had to explain to Harry why it's important to other people to say hello – it makes them think of you as a friendly person and, when they say hello to you, they're being friendly, so if you don't do it, it makes you seem unfriendly. So then he started saying hello. But he couldn't understand hugs. I asked him to give his grandma a hug because she really likes it and it makes her feel like you really like her. And people feel really nice when you give them a hug – and that's where I went wrong, he hugged everybody. I realized, okay, I need to be more specific!

BEHAVING WELL

Ask your child to shade any of the boxes they think 'it's good to':

Go to bed when I'm told to	Take things from shops without paying	Sit quietly when the teacher is talking	Keep my clothes on when I'm outside
Chew with my mouth shut	Swear when I am at school	Say thank you for presents	Clean my teeth every day
Go to the toilet in the street	Take turns and share	Have a wash to keep clean every day	Throw a tantrum if I lose a game
Say hello and goodbye to people	Draw on the walls	Stare and point at people who are different	

Use this to talk about what they feel they can master already, and what you might agree they need a bit of help with.

(We've left a blank space in case you want to add one that you have particular trouble with or want to concentrate on. And of course you could write your own list to fit with your child's ability, maturity level and your own family values.)

What we're trying to illustrate here is that children may not be too sure about what's socially acceptable or not. Getting on with people relies on the ability to practise restraint, to hold back the urge to do or say things which are likely to upset people or get them into trouble, but it's learned.

> I tell him that if he shouts at people every time he feels angry with them, he won't get on with them. So we talked about how he might let off steam another way.

You cannot single-handedly make a child understand and stick within boundaries overnight. But you can do a good job trying, especially if you call on the noble truth of enlisting. It's worth making sure everyone, in and outside your home, is giving your child the same message. You need a united front. Lots of parents tell us about how their best efforts are undermined because they haven't been able to negotiate a consistent approach.

> It wasn't enough that his class teacher knew how to handle him, the dinner ladies and the caretaker needed to know. He wandered out of school. It could have been avoided but it took that happening a few times before they realized they did need to make all the staff aware. From then on when they saw him leaving the school, they stopped him because they realized he was a child who shouldn't be on his own.

> They went away with Cubs for the night and they all got very excited. The staff thought that if you let them stay up until 10.30 p.m. they'd be tired and go to sleep. But for the kids coming out off medication, they were just flying. That's really taught me that it's just not the one teacher but the whole staff who need to be aware.

All children test the boundaries. Rebelling against limits, working out who they are and becoming more independent are part and parcel of growing up and it's even more complicated for children with complex needs. What you try might not work but it might not get any worse either, which is a coping strategy in itself! Hang onto your hope that something will eventually stick.

> Are the grown ups in charge in my house or is one small ten-year-old boy in charge? It's amazing what a slippery slope you can get into if you don't sort the boundaries for everyone.

Being brave

Sweaty palms? Feeling sick in your tummy? Blurting a few words out that don't make a lot of sense? Finding it difficult to make eye contact?

This description fits both of us when we're scared of facing something we'd really prefer to avoid, but that we knew we'd be better off facing up to. Does it sound familiar to you? From the outside, people who seem brave look like they're dealing with things heroically, with good sense, good heart and good humour. But we know that on the inside it can be completely unnerving. So why bother?

First, facing up to things that are difficult can make us feel better about ourselves.

I've noticed that I'll duck and dive to save myself the brain damage and aggravation. But I actually did confront his real problems. It wasn't a quick fix, but I decided it was okay. It was a big hurdle for me but I felt quite pleased I'd done it.

Part of feeling better about ourselves is recognizing that we can have an effect on the world, and can influence other people – remember back to our discussion earlier about developing an internal locus of control? Being brave enables us to experience that, and to confront our personal power, instead of passively relying on other people to sort everything out for us. For children with complex needs this can be an especially important lesson because, as we've discussed a lot in this book, we can fall into the trap of doing too much for them. We often want to save them as much pain as we can. Being brave invites us to help children face their uncomfortable, scared feelings, and to actively work with them.

And good things can happen as a result of being brave, things that you thought were never possible. Think how rewarding it would be to witness your nine-year-old finally plucking up the courage to go in a public toilet cubicle on their own, without you having to worry about keeping an eye on them and your other kids all at once.

So how do you go about awakening the bravery that exists in us all? An important thing you can do here is to think of yourself as a coach. If you just tell kids they're being stupid wimps, it might help you let off steam for a minute, but it won't help them in the slightest. Also, if you get so involved with what's happening that you end up trying to take all their worries away, and doing the work for them, that won't help either. What does help is if you can encourage them to believe they can sort things, even if you don't quite believe it yourself. So we might often have to take a leap of faith. And as with all the potions, we need to take a good look at ourselves and how brave we're being.

I noticed I was completely avoiding certain places because I was worried he'd behave badly. So I decided to go slowly and get back out there – starting with short trips, distracting myself so I didn't get too nervous myself, for example writing a shopping list, taking a pack of cards, a magazine – basically braving it out! And in the beginning, I made sure I left while his behaviour was okay. I was building up slowly to being able to cope with a full-blown tantrum in the supermarket.

Here are some ideas to try with your child:

- **'Be brave' message**: If they're anxious, give them a 'be brave' message. Write it on a slip of paper so they can pull it out when they need it.

- **Teddy bear**: Give them what psychologists call a 'transitional object'. Traditionally this was a teddy, but it could be anything practical. A photo of someone they find comforting, or a small object belonging to someone they like and trust (don't let them steal it), for example. The idea here is that they associate the photo or object with that person, and then it is a little bit like having them there beside them, and they then feel calmer or better able to face up to something tricky.

- **Fake it till you make it**: Children who seem scared of everything, and have little energy to change that, can be encouraged to think they can fake it until they make it. Getting your child to act as though they were confident and resilient, even if they feel that they're not, can be very effective, but you may have to try the idea a few times before it sticks.

- **Transplanting**: Get your child to remember back to a time they were brave, and help them transplant the feeling, and the skills they used, to their current situation. If your child can't think of anything, try to remember something you noticed they did themselves. You may have to be creative.

No doubt you've got more things you could add to this list, and you may have already experimented with everything on ours. But, even if you have tried these things, it can be worth giving it a bit of distance and trying again. The beauty of children growing up (even very gradually) is that opportunities keep coming back to try something that at one time they weren't ready for – so be brave, and give it another go!

Solving problems

We have a problem with problem-solving which we thought we should come clean about before we unravel what this idea means for building children's resilience. Throughout, we've promoted the value of getting familiar with each of the RT potions in your own life, in order to then apply them to children. So we wouldn't be surprised if, at this point, you were thinking that anyone raising a child with complex needs will already know loads about problem-solving. We certainly see plenty of parents and workers hunting for solutions on a pretty unrelenting basis. The tension for us is this. While it can often be better to approach a problem head on, we think it's also true that stepping back can create space for solutions to arrive.

It seems to us that all too often we end up thinking that if there's a problem we or someone, somewhere, has to fix it, and fast. We lose our perspective and even our sense of humour in a dogged determination to get to the bottom of some mess or other. Somehow, we take on the entire responsibility for making things better!

> I am so used to that manic state of desperately trying to find answers to their problems, I wouldn't know how to stop. I've been doing it for so long.

But sitting with the 'not knowing' and feeling uncomfortable about not having solutions is, in our experience, part of the territory of raising children with complex needs. It can take some of the pressure off. Getting used to living with uncertainty is a solution in itself. While we obviously all want things to be better for children, sometimes it can make sense to lighten up and relax with wherever they are and whoever they are. You cannot fix everything. Sure, remaining stuck with a problem, without a plan, can wear you down. And once you start taking a bit of action, you can end up feeling better about things almost immediately. But it's equally important to take a break from worrying and problem-solving sometimes. So having got that out of the way, what does problem-solving involve for children?

Essentially it's about helping children to assess the type and size of a problem, what they need to do to resolve it, and how they might work out who can help if necessary. It's an important skill but, more often than not, it's learned. While it might seem like you have a child who is just born with the ability to unpack situations and deal with whatever's thrown at them, chances are they've picked up some clues instinctively by watching those around them.

For example, encouraging your child to be inquisitive and getting them to ask lots of questions is one way of helping them to discover answers for themselves. Just exploring open-ended questions, you know, those ones that start with 'how' rather than 'why' and that generate more than 'yes/no' answers, can set a tone of curiosity in your home, without you even realizing it. 'What did you do at school today?' is likely to get you more information than 'Was school good today?'

In the next chapter, Core Self, we concentrate on helping children to see that their problems and who they are can be separated out, but in this Coping potion we're trying to help children find ways to solve the problems they face. Getting a child to identify their strengths and existing troubleshooting skills can be a good starting point. If you think back to the noble truth of Conserving, you might want to help them see that the clever way they dealt with one problem could hold a few hints for how to deal with another one they're struggling with. Try it on yourself.

COPY CATS

Think of a situation when someone else saw you deal with a problem well.

It doesn't have to be anything major, just a small ordinary situation that called for a few problem-solving skills on your part.

- What was the problem?
- Who saw you manage it well?
- What did they see you do?

Being focused and organized, generating alternative solutions and being flexible about how we think about things are all problem-solving skills that children can learn – even if it takes a bit of patience! Have a look at these four ideas.

Idea 1: Being focused and organized

Focusing on one problem at a time can help avoid getting overwhelmed with the size of things. Exploring and clarifying problems in detail can help organize things into manageable-sized chunks.

> Lists! I always start with a list…from the teeniest thing up. Especially when I am feeling overwhelmed – then I methodically work through it, one thing at a time. The added bonus is the lovely satisfaction of seeing it all ticked off at the end.

For very specific problems, you often have to understand the problem first. When we feel stressed or worried about our children, we can end up thinking in very fixed ways about them and we forget to stop and examine the problem and instead rush in with a knee-jerk reaction. You could try unpicking the triggers and consequences with them to figure out the meaning behind their behaviour.

Idea 2: Being able to come up with different solutions

There's rarely only one way to solve a problem so anything you can do to highlight a child's potential for finding different solutions is worth the effort.

And here's where the power of positive thinking comes in! We have to believe it's possible. Thinking they'll never sleep through at night, wash themselves, behave well, sets them and us up to fail. If we have strong beliefs that children can or cannot do certain things, we're more likely to relate to them in a way that will make them go on behaving in this way.

It can also be worth standing back and taking note of how your child goes about dealing with problems themselves, because they might do it differently to you. For example, do they ditch their first approach and try another way, do they slow things down into smaller steps, do they stop and start over, do they leave it and then come back to it later, or maybe they talk themselves through it? Leaving them to get on with it in their own way might be all that's needed but you could offer one of these as alternative suggestions when the timing is right!

Exploring the pros and cons of different options is frequently recommended by the problem-solving gurus. If you're not used to this technique, we've found dividing a page into two columns each with a pros or cons heading can graphically illustrate whether one option has stronger benefits than another. Either one column fills up or it doesn't!

> When they say 'I can't do this, it won't work' we say in our house 'it's not I can't because, it's I can if'. It drives the boys mad because they're naturally lazy. They'd prefer someone to come and fix it. It forces them to go 'Oh, now I've got to think about it, then do something about it'. Tough stuff.

Idea 3: Being flexible about how we think

Another way of approaching problems is to think about what the preferred situation would be like. Have an end in mind. For example, for the child who's getting into trouble because they're not getting their homework done, what would it be like to have it done and handed in without worrying about it? If a child has thought about and pictured what it would feel like to be on time with their work, they are more likely to keep going with ways of solving the problem until they achieve the outcome they want.

> If I've got to build a wall I imagine what it will look like and I work backwards from there. I get a picture in my mind, and often I just sketch it out, and then I deconstruct it. I break it down into smaller stages from beginning to end.

The other part of this technique is to think about what gets in the way of achieving the preferred situation. We all have thought-patterns that trip us up at times. For example, not believing we can manage our children's outbursts or their constant need for reassurance. Getting anxious about your child's behaviour can undermine your confidence and make you feel like you're a rubbish parent. How we think affects how we feel, affects how we behave. So if you go into a situation thinking you're going to fail chances are you will.

Idea 4: Make a declaration

Maybe using the ancient technique of 'affirmation' could work for you? This is about making a positive judgement about yourself and training your mind to really believe it's possible. Reciting every morning for a week 'I can manage my child, I feel in control and can cope, I am staying calm while they kick off' just might help you believe you are managing to parent your child well enough.

In our experience it certainly helps to try and see problems as an opportunity! Here comes the resilient spin. While we know it can feel like a child is deliberately making your life difficult, seeing problems more as a chance to think about how you can help them to do things differently will sustain your optimism. Problems are both a chance to learn more about a child's strengths and vulnerabilities and a chance to practise coping skills that get cemented for ongoing use. The last thing you want to get into is that wretched spiral of feeling a victim in the face of so much to deal with. Believe us, we've been there. Sorry if we sound a bit harsh, but we're not very good at stomaching too much misery or self-pity, preferring to deal with difficult situations with a touch of humour. We don't think there's a lot of point dwelling on the stuff we can't do much about.

Good problem-solvers can negotiate solutions by themselves and with others. They can find creative or humorous ways out of situations and they have the persistence to stay with a problem until it's solved. But with children with complex needs, it really doesn't do to speak too soon about problems being done and dusted. If you're in that place of fire fighting, and only just managing to paper the cracks, don't despair. Remember, you don't have to solve everything but you might have to learn to tolerate feelings of uncertainty and ambiguity.

> By stopping worrying you can free yourself up – and sometimes the answers just pop into your head because you've made the space for them to arrive.

Rose-tinted glasses

We reckon everyone could do with seeing the world through rose-tinted glasses every now and then. We all have experience of situations when imagining the more pleasant and positive parts of tricky times gets us through.

> Tom took off all his clothes in the store. I wish the ground had opened up and swallowed me, I was so embarrassed. But the amazing thing was, he'd done it so quickly! He usually takes ages at home to get ready for bathtime, so now I know he's just stalling.

Rose-tinted glasses is about putting a resilient spin on things. It's about looking at bad things that have happened and adding a positive twist to them.

The idea is a bit different to becoming an optimist, which we talk about in the next chapter, Core Self. The rose-tinted glasses idea is more about deliberately adopting a stance that helps make sense of something from the past in a positive way. You might be thinking this sounds a bit odd, because how can you make miserable things seem okay? So, just to be clear, the glasses don't get worn all the time. They get donned when needed. You don't bother with them when you could do with seeing clearly and accurately. Some situations need to be faced squarely. Some

moods just have to be endured because facing things can make them less scary, and they provide insights into what needs attention and what has to happen next. So the trick is to put your glasses on only when you need them.

Here's an example. Kim was a battered wife once, many moons ago when she lived in Australia. So, in the thick of it, it would not have helped to have used the rose-tinted glasses approach – she'd still be in the same situation! But, looking back, she says it's helped her heaps. It's fine-tuned her radar for violent situations and ways to defuse conflict, she knows something more about her part in what happened and she better understands how it is for others who lose their power. Doing what psychologists call 'reframing' this past experience has built her resilience.

Using the rose-tinted glasses idea is about helping children to construct their past experiences in the best light possible. But children with little self-worth are likely to need help to find the more resilient angle on their experience.

One useful thing you could do is to get your children to reflect on their past experiences and explore what they think those experiences were about for them. From here, you're looking to help them attach a resilient storyline to all or parts of what they're telling you. For example, we mentioned in Chapter 1, Basics, that some children want to move away from constructing their identity as 'disabled people'. While this may be a positive choice for them, they can still recognize their impairment and their experience of difference as something they have learned from and accept, and include in the blend of circumstances that make up their unique sense of self.

Putting on rose-tinted glasses, like all the ideas within the Coping potion, is about managing life rather than changing it. It offers another lens through which children can make sense of or develop a more adaptive view of their lives. So even though you might have to suggest another way of talking or thinking about things, chances are you are modelling the technique will rub off.

> She was all upset because she wished we could all live together. She wanted her dad and her mum under the same roof with her. I think reminding her that it's best for people to live where they're happiest and that she has two places where she belongs helped a little bit.

The other thing you could do is encourage your child to share their stories about themselves with others. It's a way of helping them define themselves in a positive light, resiliently. You could even set up situations with this in mind. Kim remembers staging *This is Your Life* shows for family occasions, with her younger sister. They always got a laugh. Maybe get your child to rehearse it with you first, so you can be sure to check for the resilient twist.

You might be thinking this is all a bit peculiar because you already have a child who has a false picture of their lives so you don't want to encourage any more improbable ideas. Rose-tinted glasses is only one way of framing what is happening.

> Nick has no sense of danger. He used to think he was Superman and so could run in the middle of the road and jump off cliffs. His brother told him it was rubbish, but he really believed he wouldn't get splattered.

It's not a matter of encouraging delusions of grandeur. While some children may have an unrealistic notion of their capabilities, more often than not they reveal astonishingly low self-esteem and are brilliant at self-criticism. Putting a resilient spin on things could mean tempering their enthusiasm and thinking more in terms of working towards becoming grand! Even if they don't make it, they'll never actually fail because they'll always be having a crack at getting there.

So next time you feel like raising your kids is maddening, upsetting and even boring, see if you can find those glasses – the rose-tinted ones of course!

> Putting rose-tinted glasses on when I feel sad can cheer me right up.

Foster their interests

This idea is a bit of a sideways move in the Coping potion. It involves doing fun things that may not have anything to do with what children are struggling with. But fostering children's interests promotes resilience for a number of reasons.

It can give children opportunities to succeed and as a result their self-esteem improves and they have fun, meaning the quality of their lives improves. Succeeding helps children feel as though they are in control of their lives. Remember our discussion of developing an internal locus of control? Even if children aren't particularly good at what they're interested in, they can enjoy it anyway, which makes them feel happier and as a result stronger and more able to deal with difficulties that come their way. The therapeutic effects of having fun should never be underestimated.

> Once I discovered how much he enjoys comedy, we made efforts to watch programmes together, then we'd share the experience of laughing together, and retell the jokes to one another on grumpy days.

> To be strong and know I could cope with looking after my kids with all their problems meant I needed to feel happy. So I sorted my week so that there were times when I focused on me. I did what I liked and what I wanted to do.

Children can learn to lose themselves in activities they enjoy, irrespective of how well they do them, which also helps strengthen their ability to be by themselves and to be less reliant on others.

Fostering their interests can also get children out and about and in turn gives them more opportunities to be affected by other resilient things that may happen. This then can set up chains of positive reactions that you might never have anticipated. For example, your child likes football, but isn't particularly good at it. She goes to a special needs football club, and meets someone who tells her about the mainstream karate class they're doing. Her dad gets her into that class, staying with her for a few weeks until it's clear she can cope on her own. They discover that she's actually really good at karate, and she manages to get a medal for it, as well as carrying on enjoying the football class too.

And fostering children's interests can simply give everyone a rest from focusing on trying to change difficult things.

So set yourself the task of noticing what your child gets interested in. And then look back at the Basics and Belonging, Chapters 1 and 2, where we give more ideas on getting them involved in things. The other point here is to have an open mind yourself. Encourage your child to try anything that seems remotely realistic.

If your child is a bit obsessive, it's worth having a go at getting them to channel that obsession into something positive (like swimming), rather than watching the same DVD over and over again. If that seems far too ambitious, you could try to get them to do more creative things with the particular obsession they have. Trains is an obvious one here.

You can only visit the Bluebell steam railway line soooo many times!

Irritating though obsessions are, trains are at least a useful transport option to get to places. And you could expand your child's transport interests by taking your bikes on a train and cycling off into the country-side. They can also draw trains, bake them as cakes, and download train routes and timetables.

Fostering children's interests is a good thing to do in its own right because it helps build resilience. But it can also be a springboard to noticing the things children do well and the areas in their lives where they show real talent and creativity at managing difficulties. It can give you a real buzz to see your child doing something fun, and you might even find a new interest for yourself. Anyone for tennis?

The satisfaction on his face makes the whole thing worthwhile.

Calming down

My three react to stress in very different ways. One gets really anxious and worries about the world, the middle one starts acting out and gets stroppy and argumentative and the older one, because of his ASD, deals with it by bombarding me with questions.

All children get in a state from time to time, but some of us live with kids who are like it day in, day out. Our children can get angry, upset or scared by particular things that wouldn't bother other kids so much, if at all. Others are just constantly worked up, excessively excited or on the go all day. And some obsess constantly about one thing over and over. Whichever way they do it, they're exhausting to be around, but the good news is that they can be helped to calm down.

Tapping into where, when and, if possible, why your child gets worked up can give you some useful pointers to helping them to calm down.

If you found this exercise a bit tricky, don't worry, as it can take time to get in the habit of noticing these kinds of things. But looking for

---

WHAT MAKES YOUR CHILD GET IN A STATE?

Jot down a few of the situations that you know they get worked up about. Try to remember where and when it happened:

Now experiment with reasons why they might have got in a state at that particular time and place:

1.

2.

3.

---

reasons can be quite interesting – you might even feel a bit like a detective, trying to get to the bottom of something. And while it might often seem like there is no reason, it might be something you don't realize, like their blood sugar levels being out of balance or something might have happened to upset them when you weren't around. Of course you won't always be able to solve the riddle, but if you do, and you can change something quite simply, it will have been worth putting in the effort to think about it.

It's always worth trying to get your child to notice when, where and why they get in a state. So you could try the exercise you've just done with them and see if the two of you have come up with the same ideas. If not, you might need to swap a few more thoughts to see if you can find some common ground.

Once you both have a bit of an idea about where, when and why they get in a state, you could try to help them understand their own role in what happens. Look back at what we've said about developing an internal locus of control. You're trying to help them work towards being able to feel something very deeply (anger, sadness, anxiety) but act differently. If they practise acting differently, eventually their feelings will change too, and they will calm down. This is all about helping them to be more in control of themselves.

> When we go to the cinema Emily needs to know where the exits are in case she has to get out in a hurry and when she's with a crowd she has to know where the adults are in case she needs protecting from some imagined danger.

It's likely you will have to try different things before you stumble on what works. There are lots of books and DVDs available that provide strategies for calming down. We've learnt that the important thing is not to give up too soon. A child might refuse to use a relaxation tape on one day but do it on another. And if they're very reluctant, you could introduce the idea of research to them. Tell them that whatever it is you want to try has been proved to work or not work, so you'd be interested in their opinion on the matter. Would they be willing to try it out?

For those children who are extremely anxious and edgy, we have the following ideas:

- Use 'positive self-talk' instead of imagining the worst.

- Help them anticipate stressful situations and plan ahead by organizing low-stress visits to get familiar with new places or people.

- Distract them from whatever's causing the anxiety by giving them something else to do and think about.

- Agree a visual cue with your child that reminds them of calmness.

- Use the 'teddy bear' idea we mentioned earlier so they associate a calm person (maybe that's you) with an object they carry with them.

- Remind them to breathe deeply or telephone you if they're out on their own.

- Don't avoid the situation but break it down into smaller steps or introduce elements of what's worrying them gradually.

- Make sure they're eating, exercising and sleeping well because worrying all the time can be exhausting so exercise will increase their energy.

And for those children who need help with anger you could try these suggestions:

- Karate, punch bags, banging away on percussion instruments.

- Screaming and shouting in a room away from other people.

- Leaving the room.

- Distracting them with something completely different.

- Having a bath with bubbles to distract them.

- Stroking themselves or a pet (not a fish!).

- Humming or whistling.

- Cuddling a toy or even you if you're lucky.

And what about massage, singing and meditation? We know that massage can relieve muscle tension and lots of people use it for relaxation as well as managing stress and anxiety. Some schools have introduced it as part of their morning routine. It's a healing instinct to rub an aching arm or a sore head, so intuitively we suspect it satisfies our basic need to be touched. Plus it works in the same way as exercise, providing natural pain relief as it releases endorphins, which are anti-stress hormones that block pain signals to your brain. There's also some persuasive evidence relating to the benefits of baby massage on early mother–child relationships and postnatal depression (Zealey 2005).

So it's not surprising that many people believe it improves bonding and attachment too.

I went to a baby massage class and I swear he started to sleep better.

So, as there's no evidence that it's damaging in any way, we'd like to promote it to you as a form of nurturing touch that feels good anyway. Go for it.

And why not consider singing? There is some research suggesting that singing not only improves mood but also strengthens the immune system. It's used by lots of people as a therapy for relaxation, depression and anxiety and it's often a quick way to release energy and escape the strain of stressful situations. But we don't mean pushing children to stand up in front of audiences to perform – which is one of Kim's less happy childhood memories. We mean the singing we do secretly in the shower or car, or for all to hear in church or at the football match. Singing is already natural to most of us as we've probably all sung for pleasure at some time or other and we know how it can affect our moods. It's a simple, easy and free technique for calming down. Just listening to that old song 'Somewhere Over the Rainbow' can make us at least feel part of the universe, so how powerful is that! While she hated the per-forming, Kim's fondest childhood memory is her mum singing because it dissolved the tension in the house somehow.

She's only 12 but when she's glum I think about a piece of music I know she loves. I put it on without telling her and get on with the chores. I'm trying to get her to push through. It's hard to feel weak if you're singing along to 'We are the champions, my friend...'

See if you can get more music in your life. Whether it's singing off key, humming or whistling along to the radio blissfully unaware of who's lis-tening, it's like natural voice therapy that can keep you in a calm place when things are looking a bit bleak.

And our final suggestion, meditation? Lots of people swear by its power to help you relax and ease the tension of living. And it's generally recognized as being one of the most beneficial things you can do to create a powerful and positive mind. It's a way of getting out of the usual way of thinking about things into a deeper state of awareness. A bit like sitting down with yourself in the here and now, so you begin to notice your thoughts and actions or motivations in a clearer way. In our experi-ence it can certainly help loosen your grip so you can think bigger. There are lots of different techniques and, while we can't explain them here, it's not hard to find books and organizations that will teach you and even provide places for practice. And some schools are including it as part of assembly time! You don't have to sit cross-legged and chant to meditate. Regular 20-minute walks alone are like a mini-meditation. Not surprising then that people from different cultures throughout time have gone on walking journeys as a path to self-discovery!

And just as you need to help your children understand what triggers their anger or anxiety, you need to get familiar with what happens for you. Time and time again we meet parents who are so caught up in helping their children they're neglecting their own health and getting themselves wound up with the demands of it all. Find a quiet place and conjure up one really good memory of doing something you love. Make an agreement with yourself to come back to that memory when you're het up. It's been proven that this approach can really calm people. And helping your child to find an event or time from the past when they experienced success, or when they managed to calm themselves down, will remind them that they can do it again too.

We asked the parents who helped with this book what they did to calm down when things got too much. Here's a few of their suggestions:

> I hadn't realized that my morning shower routine builds my strength. It helps me catch a few quiet moments alone before starting the day and sets me up to be slightly more calm (which isn't very calm of course). So now I've put a resilient spin on it – I suddenly noticed I already do things that I can build on.

> Self-talk is really important to me. No one else wants to talk with me! Just joking. I say to myself, 'Excuse me, I want to throw something', and that's enough, I don't start throwing!

> I had this toothache banging away. I'd agreed to see this show and I was that close to not going and thinking I really just want to curl up in my bed (I even almost wanted my mother, but not quite) and I went and we had a fantastic time, I laughed and laughed. Sometimes it's worth just pushing yourself a little. It's so easy to say I can't be bothered.

The great thing is, calming down can be contagious. If your child sees you creating space to self-soothe and relax when things are tense, they'll pick up the message. What you do can spill over onto them.

> He says 'I can't do this right now' and goes to his room and puts himself in a time out, to calm down, and then he'll come back and for that he gets praised. We taught him to do this when he was in a rage

---

CHILLING OUT

Think about the things you do practically or mentally and see if you can fill in the following:

One thing that winds me up

One way I let off steam

One thing that calms me down

---

but it's kind of the first time he's really thought to use it in other areas of difficulty. He just goes off and leaves because it's all too much. And I think that's really good, he's done really well to do that.

Tomorrow is another day

If you're the sort of person who never bears a grudge and can serenely move on from every hideous situation you find yourself in, then by all means gloat a bit first, but move on to the next section. For the rest of us, trying to develop the skill of remembering that tomorrow is another day, and acting calm and dignified, may not come so naturally.

> Thankfully I caught myself in the mirror. Not a pretty sight! I was screaming and swearing, my hair was standing on end, my face was all red, and I looked like a wild banshee. Even my child looked more normal than me. I pulled myself together and took a deep breath, and remembered that maybe tomorrow things will be different, and I'll have another chance to feel in control and sorted.

Really managing to remember that tomorrow is another day helps us find a solid place to stand, and then we're not so overwhelmed by our emotions in the present moment. We can think carefully about how to respond, rather than just flailing around. We can improvise if we need to, and be much more creative about solving problems. Also, it can get us out of that spiral of negative thinking that so many of us can understandably get into. Remember the idea of being open to the possibility of turning negative chain reactions into positive ones with just one small resilient move? This might be easier said than done, but here are a few ideas about how to get into the mindset. Use them with your child or on yourself first if you like.

Notice how much time you spend and energy you waste being cross and resentful about what has happened. Then give yourself a specific time and place to vent your feelings. Other than that, be very disciplined with yourself about replacing resentful thoughts with different thoughts. It can help to train yourself to think about something quite specific, but nice – your favourite chocolate cake recipe for example.

Remember, the great and wonderful thing is that hardly anything seems as bad when you think back to it, a few weeks (or years!) down the line.

Write yourself a message and keep it by your bed: 'Just hold on in there – this time will pass, it always does.'

As we keep on saying, the RT ideas work well together, so go for a massive attack – calm down, put on rose-tinted glasses, and follow the example of this parent, remembering that tomorrow's another day.

> I cut my son's hair but wasn't paying attention and I put the wrong clipper attachment on – it was seriously short. I thought, oh no, how am I going to get him to cope with this when he goes to school tomorrow. Even though he didn't want to go because he said the other kids would laugh, he decided that tomorrow's another day and someone else will have done something stupid by then and he won't be the butt of everyone's jokes.

Lean on others

Leaning on others is related but different to our noble truth of enlisting. Deciding to lean on others means that you're probably not going to be as in control of the situation as you would be if you're enlisting. This is not about organizing and co-ordinating others but about leaning on them for help.

It's about giving yourself the opportunity to take a step back and protect yourself, because maybe you just can't manage at the moment.

> I've chosen to back off and get more outside help, because I now accept that she just won't listen to me any more.

> I was completely worn out and couldn't think straight. I needed someone to just come in and take over for a bit.

Of course being in this situation can make you feel very vulnerable. So it's important to lean on people you think you'll be able to trust. However, sometimes it's a compromise.

> We're facing so many big changes, so I had the social workers in – we came out on the risk rating 4 out of 4 and 5 out of 5 on the relationship breakdown – I'm standing on the edge of collapse – I had to do a quick flip on that because this means they are going to do something for him, and never mind me the failing mum in the corner.

Take a big breath, and fake it till you make it. Perhaps you'll never feel completely comfortable getting other people involved like this, and for good reason. As parents we've both had tricky times with professionals when we'd wished we'd never bothered asking for help, and then other times when people have almost saved our sanity. So on balance, we think leaning on others can help you get a bit of distance from the situation, so you can come at it afresh. It also can help other people really understand what it is you're coping with – you might even end up slightly gloating when they don't manage to sort out everything either!

There's no shame in accepting that you can lose the ability to assess what should happen next and need to trust others to get involved at times. This goes for children too. Some are very trusting, and naturally lean on others, perhaps more than we think they should. Others are scared to do so and need help to shift away from using their own judgements and instincts to trusting and relying on yours, or other adults'. So talk about this with your child. See if you can help them come up with people they could lean on a bit for help with specific things. One way of doing this is to get your child to draw around their hand and write the names of people who can help them on each of the fingers and thumb. Encourage them to pick one, and try it out, if necessary.

> I was surprised when my kids said they'd go to this woman I know who doesn't have any kids, if they were in trouble. It made me take care of that relationship a bit more. And when I told her that they viewed her as a safe person, she was so thrilled.

Conclusion

Children need to learn to manage the demands of life in ways that work for them rather than against them. So assisting them to understand and apply the remedies in this chapter – stick to boundaries, be brave, solve problems, wear rose-tinted glasses if necessary, foster their talents, calm down when they're anxious or angry, remember that tomorrow is another day and lean on others if they have to – will build their resilience.

We might want big changes which would instantly make raising our children easier. But it's unlikely to happen like that. Before you get too depressed, remember the little things we do can end up having a big effect on our ability to manage day to day. The good news is that coping is about working on the outside, and that's easier to change than anything else. So while it may take patience and a willingness to try different things, behaviour is much more open to being changed than a child's deep inner feelings. So there's a big possibility of success with this one if you really stick at it.

As parents, we are in a great position (when we're not too tired) to guide children to understand more about their interactions with the world and to develop more control. Modelling positive coping styles – so actually looking like you're calm and are managing, when you actually feel like hitting the roof – can really help. However you go about it, helping them believe they can have an impact on their own lives and the lives of others, is a very resilient thing to do.

So now you've read what's involved in the Coping potion, can you see how it might apply to yourself?

TAKE THE COPING TEST

	Yes	No	Sometimes
I can set boundaries and stick to what I say without being pushed around by my child	☐	☐	☐
I can stand up for myself when others are unfairly criticizing me	☐	☐	☐
I can find ways to solve some of the problems that I face	☐	☐	☐
I can imagine things are better than they are if I have to	☐	☐	☐
I know what my interests are and I give myself the opportunity to follow them	☐	☐	☐
I can calm myself down when I feel like I'm going to lose it	☐	☐	☐
I can get things in perspective and remember things won't always be how they feel in the moment	☐	☐	☐
I can ask someone to help me when I need it	☐	☐	☐

We hope that doing this has provided a few clues about what you do well already and what you might want to work on a bit more. And now, after a recap, to the final potion, Core Self.

Let's recap
Coping – this potion helps children to get by in everyday life.

- Understand boundaries and keep to them.

- Be brave.

- Solve problems.

- Put on rose-tinted glasses.

- Foster their interests.
- Calm her/himself down, self-soothe.
- Remember that tomorrow is another day.
- elp child to lean on others when necessary.

CHAPTER 5

CORE SELF

I think it's kind of about your beliefs and all the rest of it, isn't it?

It's the bit that makes you, you.

In the RT book written for a professional audience, Angie and Derek wrote a chapter exploring what they meant by the Core Self potion, and giving some ideas about how they felt the idea could be put to use in practice. Angie remembers it being one of the hardest chapters to write because the ideas aren't easy to grasp, let alone convey to others.

We've learnt from parents that the term 'core self' isn't immediately obvious. It's not the language they use or automatically apply to family life. Instead, they told us they tend to think about their children's self-esteem and their confidence and they used terms like 'being true to yourself' and 'in touch with who you are'.

This is, in fact, exactly what we mean. Core Self is about the personal ideas, beliefs and assumptions that children have in relation to themselves. Its focus is on understanding who you are, and then building internal, personal strengths because how a child feels about themselves affects their approach to life. With Core Self there really are no quick fixes and no simple tips to try that will have an instant effect. Core Self, in many ways, forces us to acknowledge how hard it is to raise children with complex needs, and what a long-term approach we need to take to change the way they are in a deep and lasting way. This is quite a tough thing to say this far into the book, and we realize that you may not have been able to take on many of the suggestions offered so far anyway, let alone the ones we are about to discuss in this chapter, given all the things you might be dealing with in your life.

Of all the RT potions, Core Self is perhaps the most demanding when it comes to parents being reflective and self-aware. There are a few reasons for this. First, getting to know ourselves – what makes us tick and function – is not always that easy. Funny to think that, given that the only person who is with us 24 hours a day is ourselves. Second, you might be the sort of person who really doesn't see the point in thinking about this kind of thing. You just are who you are. Third, if you get to know yourself, there is the possibility that you might not like what you find, and that can be painful to acknowledge. You might, quite rightly, be worried that you're opening a can of worms. And finally, if you don't like some of what you find, taking on board the idea of change is often very unsettling and hard work. Phew, what a list! And that's before you even start thinking about your children.

We think that accepting and even loving yourself and at the same time being open to change is a tension that's worth getting used to living with. Because, fortunately, many of the ideas we have for working with children's Core Self are also worth trying out directly on yourself. In a nutshell, the challenge is about encouraging children and young people to like who they are, know their own abilities, believe in their own worth and value, and at the same time be open to changing those bits that don't serve them well.

The ideas we're suggesting you might like to apply in Core Self work are a bit of a mixed bag. Some are straightforward things to do with kids. Others are best shared with children by modelling them yourself – so less about doing things to and with children and more about a way of being and an attitude to how you raise them as people. It's about adding or turning up the emotional dimension and language to your parenting style.

The reminder we keep coming back to, of course, is to be aware of your child's age and capabilities so you don't expose them to challenges for which they're not developmentally ready. Much of what we are suggesting in this chapter are illustrations of ideas that will require some adaptation on your part to best suit the particular abilities and situations of the children you care about.

The bottom line is that all of the ideas in this chapter rely on us having a 'can do' approach that encourages children to believe in themselves and imparts the possibility of choice and change and, as it's the last of the five potions, we're guessing that you might be like us and find it hard to get into a self-conscious mindset that concentrates on children's emotional territory. Don't give up just yet – because we think Core Self is a really rich and lush potion.

PONDERING

Think of something, an activity, that you've done in the last few weeks with your child.

Now list the things you did to help him or her to stay positive and relaxed about the activity.

You've just been reflective!

The ideas we're going to talk about in this chapter are about ways we can instil a sense of hope in children and how to help them understand themselves and other people. It also includes helping children to grow into adults able to take responsibility for themselves, fostering their talents and using tried and tested treatments for specific problems.

Just like the other potions already mentioned, Basics, Belonging, Learning and Coping, the art lies in finding ways to make it happen. So the goal is to build up a child's sense of themselves, so that they feel likeable, are hopeful and optimistic, are pleased to do nice things for others, respect themselves and those around them, are willing to be responsible for what they do and are open to change. Not much of a challenge! Our guess is that the best thing to start with is the idea of hope.

Finding ways to instil a sense of hope

Hope is what we still have when it seems like everything else is taken away. It's that quality we bring to our lives that helps us hold on to the possibility of change and the anticipation and wish that tomorrow will be better. And when it's present it can make the most difficult of challenges feel manageable and survivable.

> When it seemed like my daughter might die, having hope that she wouldn't kept me stronger and helped me get through each moment. There's nothing to be lost in having hope. I could have just gone under, but hope kept me sane through an intolerable time. And I learnt that, whatever the outcome of a situation, having hope is a comfort that helps me cope in the moment. I use it a lot.

You might be thinking how naive, or that this isn't my way. It may be that who your child is or how they're behaving at the moment makes it impossible to imagine how you could ever instil a sense of hope in them, let alone top it up in yourself. Take note now: as two people who live with and observe the challenges parents deal with, and the obstacles children with complex needs handle, instilling a sense of hope can take time. And it can feel like we take two steps forward, only to find that we're then taking one step back. For others it comes very naturally, to people with a religious or spiritual aspect to their lives, for example:

> I do have quite a lot of spirituality – and I don't see any of that in the RT understanding of Core Self.

Although Angie and her colleague didn't write much about this in the first book about RT, we've come to think more about the place of spirituality and religious beliefs in relation to developing resilience. But we feel the need to tread a bit carefully here, because we don't want to put you off if this really isn't your thing. Nor do we want to ignore the fact that providing hope is part of the value of religious affiliations and having a strong spiritual aspect to our lives. It can be a route to gathering a sense of right and wrong and a belief in goodness and that right will win. Children who have confidence and faith in morality and goodness may well express this as a belief in God or a higher spiritual being. And it is also true that both finding a sense of hope, and having a religious or spiritual belief, have been separately and closely associated with resilience.

However, if this doesn't do it for you or you're the type of person who tends to see the glass half empty rather than half full, you might find comfort in Seligman's research. He and his team had a very high success rate in turning pessimists into optimists. How did they do it? Well, it's quite complicated to explain, but he's written a bestseller about it if you're really intrigued (Seligman 2006). We mention it because some of the ideas in his book overlap with ours. In summary, the research team did some workshop sessions, teaching assertiveness training and stress management techniques. They also showed participants how they can distract themselves from thoughts that aren't very helpful and that wear them down. So, for example, a mum continually fretting about whether her ten-year-old will ever leave home can learn the skill of shifting her mind onto another topic. One of Seligman's simple suggestions is to say 'stop' out loud to yourself when you catch yourself worrying, and shift your attention to something else. Meditation skills help you do this too. Most importantly, the research team helped people learn to argue with themselves, and to come up with their own alternatives to negative thought patterns. This idea, of changing the way you think about things, has been around in psychology for a long while now. We've already offered some ideas about how to work on this in Chapter 4, Coping. Pessimists can become optimists. But, of course, Seligman, his team and the workshop participants had to put quite a lot of work into it. And we should point out that in applying their research, as far as we know, the children they work with are from mainstream schools, so the challenges were not as great as the ones some of you might face. Helping children with complex needs to see their lives as having the potential to change and to progress may take an awful lot of effort. But as one parent suggests, it's likely that you're already more experienced at it than you think:

> Don't we acquire a lot of our resilience because we have to face these things? If nothing bounces us around the world, we wouldn't have to bounce. At least we know something about bouncing.

Locating the things that help us to move on, despite the barriers, can provide a useful clue to knowing how to assist children to discover hope for themselves. We suspect we all have experience of gloomy days when we feel stuck and powerless and we just want to hide under the covers – forever! It's awful and debilitating feeling hopeless. But what makes us shift our thinking and get a better, healthier perspective?

WHAT HELPS HOPE RETURN?

List what you have done in the past to jolt yourself out of those times when you felt miserable and hopeless.

Gaining hope is often seen as a turning point in a person's life and we know that it plays a big role in our mental health. Helping children to hang onto the idea that they will sooner or later learn this, or manage that, or that if they do this it will make a difference to that, all contribute to their getting hold of hope.

> I'm very isolated. I haven't got much outside of my kids. I suppose my kids are my life really – at the moment they need me a great deal. I would like something outside of them but I don't get that at the moment. There's hope though, I know it won't always be like this.

Hope is about the future and the possibility and promise that life can be different to how it is now, that it doesn't have to follow the expected pattern or the negative path some might have predicted. And it's probably even more important for children with complex needs because, in our experience, they are often at the receiving end of limited expectations and underestimations of their abilities.

> Sometimes I feel that everyone expects us to fail and the statistics are stacked against us. I remember reading that kids with learning difficulties and such problems are more likely to end up in prison, and me being a single parent apparently doesn't help. But then I think, given all this negativity from society, it's a miracle we're not doing so badly; in fact, when you look at it, we're doing really well.

This might all sound overly simple, especially to those of us who aren't naturally cheerful types. It's true that some people are just born with a sunny temperament while others find it really hard to shrug off worries and keep a positive outlook on things. And it's also true that many of the children we're parenting and supporting face significant obstacles. But learning to be optimistic can be worth the investment, even though getting used to concentrating on the things that work well and give children a sense of value can take practice. Have a go at the 'Feeling Good' exercise over the page, but before you do, it's even better if you can find someone else to do it with you.

> Walking in the fresh air, I know, makes me feel better, I've tried it, it works. By stopping and thinking about it, I can give myself a sense of hope.

We found that when we shared our answers with each other it helped us notice the positives and made us aware that we could choose to put more of these people, places and things in our lives. But the sense of hope we

FEELING GOOD

List the people, places or things that help you to feel uplifted and good about yourself – add more bubbles if you need them.

got from pinpointing the stuff that made us feel good also came from someone else listening to and wanting to know what our answers were. While there are moves we and our children can make for ourselves, it's highly likely that encouraging children to share their thoughts and ideas with others helps them to learn to trust that others care. It's also an opportunity for them to learn to be sensitive to the moods of others. You might like to do this exercise with your children and ask them about the things that help them to feel good about themselves.

Of course, it's the everyday happenings and experiences of daily living that provide the stage for learning about and building our Core Self. So while working on instilling a sense of hope is not particularly complicated, it does require a willingness to keep searching for ways to jump the hurdles that get in the way of our children taking part in normal and ordinary developmental opportunities.

Sometimes, the scale of the task and our own sense of incompetence can get in the way of remaining hopeful. We know those feelings of powerlessness and ineffectiveness can dog us all. Resilient therapists, remember that's us, have to be able to see what would make a difference,

believe we can and decide to get stuck in. Being convinced that there is always something we can do has a knock-on effect on the whole system. It affects us as parents and workers, it affects the children we're supporting and it affects the other adults and children involved too. Holding the hope on behalf of children might be the best we can offer in the face of distressing hardship and disadvantage.

> When I see children or parents feeling hopeless, I just say it out loud, 'I know you feel lousy about it, but I'm going to be feeling hopeful about it for you.' Or I say, 'I've seen people who've been in the same place as you right now, and they have got beyond it.'

Asking someone else to think that you're going to be okay in the face of a specific challenge can be a simple but powerful technique for instilling hope. One parent told us a story about going for a job interview. She'd woken early in the morning in order to have extra time to get herself into a calm and positive way of thinking in preparation for the interview. But when she went into the kitchen, she found that her children had emptied and trashed the contents of all the cupboards, fridge and freezer. So she rang her friend and asked her to just believe she could get through the interview. When she got there she called to mind her friend knowing she believed she would be brilliant at the job. It really helped her hold onto the possibility that she would be successful. She was! Having someone outside the situation who will listen to you talking about the latest challenges, or those times when you feel like nothing you do works, can help to separate the problems out from who we are and keep our sense of hope intact.

Now that we've set out what we mean by hope, we can go onto thinking about the other ideas in the Core Self potion. Helping a child to know her/himself is the next issue we deal with.

Helping children to know themselves

I just have never thought of myself as having that deep level. I'm quite shallow and I like it that way.

First off, like many of us, you may be thinking that you don't even know who *you* are yet, so helping your child to find out who *they* are could seem a tad ambitious. And you might be wondering why children need to know much about themselves anyway, because surely they ought to just get on with the business of being children and not worry about such serious matters so early in life?

But there are two good reasons why it's worth your while helping children to develop some awareness of who they are. In order for children to feel good about themselves they need to feel it from the inside, so that they don't have to rely on outsiders telling them all the time. And the route to feeling good from the inside is through learning about yourself – while also being confident and accepting of the fact that there are bits that you may need to change. So that brings us to the second reason: if you don't know yourself, how can you change?

For children who are brought up safe and securely, getting to know and to feel good about themselves starts early. As small children we look to significant people in our lives, like our parents, to show us that we're approved of and loved. That's why it's so important for us to cuddle and make eye contact with our babies because then the baby learns that they can light up their parents' faces with just a smile or a gurgle. They also learn through this early non-verbal communication that, if they smile or gurgle, their parent or carer will smile too, and so the baby begins to get some confirmation that they're cherished and appreciated. They begin to establish their sense of self-worth.

Children who have a strong sense of themselves often have more confidence and healthier self-esteem. And they can manage situations more successfully, because things are less overwhelming when they have some idea of the way they feel and why. Having a good sense of self-worth means managing life better.

But what about children with complex needs? Growing up safe and secure, even though parents might well be doing their very best to achieve this, is not always so simple. We think that society in general has a rather negative attitude to special needs and disability. The articles, images and stories we read in newspapers or watch on television and the conversations we hear are very often centred around a child's biological differences and deficits, their vulnerabilities or developmental delay, their dependency on others. And as researchers such as Priestley (1998), Middleton (1999) and Avery (1999) have found, it's not uncommon for people, on the whole, to talk about special needs and disability in terms of personal tragedy. We're all exposed to these ideas and unhelpful representations, so it's likely that our children are picking up aspects of these negative messages too.

It's realistic to expect that children with complex needs will often continue to need others to help them to feel worthy and good about who they are, for longer than other children do. They are likely to find life harder to handle because the way society reacts to them conspires to mean they will keep looking to the reactions of others to define themselves. They are less likely to look to their inner selves or trust their own abilities, to see them through life's difficulties. And for some kids, hard though it is to say it here, developing a strong, positive Core Self is always going to be problematic.

DID YOU KNOW...

The Disability Rights Commission Survey of young disabled people by NOP found:

- 25% felt discriminated against at school
- 49% say they missed out on PE or games at school
- 38% say they were bullied at school
- 32% say they missed out on longer trips away from school with their classmates
- 20% felt they had been discouraged.

(Disability Rights Commission 2003)

Given the social context, children with complex needs may have fewer people in their lives who can deal with their difficult feelings and experiences, and who reinforce their self-worth. Even more reason then to focus on these issues, and help them to do it for themselves. By encouraging children to spot their own strengths and weaknesses and notice what's important to them, we can help them to develop their own strong sense of identity. And by continually providing feedback and getting the other significant adults in their lives to do the same, children can grow healthy views of themselves as valued members of their families, peer groups and communities.

So, what does this all mean in practice? One of the really important tasks for us as resilient therapists is to provide children with opportunities to recognize, accept and talk about their feelings safely. It's possible that they have little idea of who they are. Actually most children probably don't think much about how others see them or how they see themselves, it's something you develop as you get older and we don't live in a society that is comfortable with talking about feelings and painful experiences. Well, not in the UK anyway. So you might have to provide an environment that makes it kind of normal to ask 'emotional questions'. If you could summon up the energy, or get a moment away from the kids, how about imagining yourself as the quiz writer for one of those popular teen magazines?

QUIZ MASTER

- What would your best friend say were your best qualities?
- How many things can you list that make you feel good about yourself?
- Which of these ten emotions have you felt in your life?
- Of these five feelings, which ones do you feel most in one week?

Hard though it can be to get the time and space to do this, it can really help to be curious about our children's lives and the views they have about themselves. This gives them the chance to practise saying what they think and feel – and it gives us the chance to put a resilient spin on their thinking if necessary!

It isn't easy to listen to children putting themselves down or being overly anxious, or talking about hating school or other people. It can help to remember that the children we're talking about may have more fragile self-esteem. Children may need to experience that the uncertainty is being held and, while we cannot always resolve what's happened, we can help a child accept things. Just giving them permission to talk about how they feel, even if it is hard to hear, can take the fear out of the feelings and it means their experiences are not denied but instead you are giving them value. And sometimes we have to accept the present and not try to make things better. What we're doing is tolerating the feelings and communicating that it's okay to feel lousy for now, for a while, and we understand it. Children may need to experience that the uncertainty is being held and, while we cannot resolve things, we can help a child accept it. On the other hand, some kids have such an unrealistic sense of who they are and what they are capable of, it can be really hard to listen without crushing their enthusiasm. The point is, right now you're just trying to practise listening to them, without actually doing anything.

> When he goes to bed, he starts – what if Mummy dies, and Daddy dies, and they all die. He goes round and round and I feel really inadequate because being a mum is about protecting him, making him feel happy, reassuring him. We tried looking at different beliefs, but he settled on Buddhism and being reincarnated...but then he worried he wouldn't recognize me because we'd both be reincarnated!

> My son has a diary by his bed – rather than shouting out continuously to me and catastrophizing, he puts the word down in the book and it gets it out of his head.

> We tried post-it notes, on her door. It puts it outside of herself and she relaxes more because she can think she's got it on the post-it note.

Luckily, what and how we parents say things is likely to make the world of difference to whether or not children pick up on the cues for getting to know themselves better. Sure, trying to help children to feel comfortable with their feelings when we might not be comfortable with our own could make for quite an entertaining comedy routine, but see if any of these ideas we've collected from parents and professionals hit the spot. And we know that training yourself to talk to kids when you're feeling fed up might require a bit of discipline. Being prepared to try things out

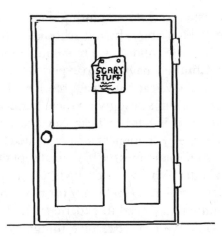

from different angles will help. Here are some ideas for talking about feelings.

1.   Have a timer and set it so that you let your child talk for ten minutes about themselves and their feelings without interrupting. It sounds easy, but you'll be amazed how hard it is. Non-directive play is a similar idea but for little ones. This is the sort of play where the child leads and you follow. So whatever they're doing, you just join in by copying or repeating some of the things they're doing or saying as they play. You don't introduce your own ideas or comments, but just take their lead. Again, time yourself, because if you're a control freak like us it'll drive you nuts.

2.   Ask your child to pretend they're making a film recording about their own life for a specific audience. It's a way to help them to stand outside of themselves a bit and increase their awareness of who they are, because they get a bit of distance and have to explain their story to other people who don't know them like you do. Or get them to make up a song about themselves or write a poem.

3.   For older children, becoming an observer can really help them explore their own feelings and reactions. Simply start using observer language; for example: 'Have you noticed when you feel worried you seem to shout a lot?' or 'I've noticed that when you're angry you want to hit things.'

4. Congratulating your child on the good choices they make, even when they are quite small. It is quite easy to do once you're in the habit of spotting them. For example: 'Deciding to wear that coat today to keep the rain off was ever so clever of you.'

5. Wondering out loud with your child in earshot is another handy technique for children who struggle to put words to their feelings or have switched off from their emotions. For example: 'I wonder how I could help him know he is lovable and clever even though he doesn't know it himself?', or 'Hmm, is this one of those moments when she feels nervous, I wonder?'

6. Have a 'let's look at the photos' event and get your child to put the images into some kind of order by date or theme.

7. Try sharing your own interests with them if you think they're remotely interested because how we feel about our pet loves isn't usually hard to talk about. Sharing your own enthusiasms out loud is an easy way to model the skill of self-awareness. Or being curious about something they're interested in could be another neutral way to practise talking about feelings. Be warned though, your love of collecting old plates may not be their passion and it's usually a good idea to avoid comparisons with others in the family, unless they're no longer around or you can do it in a positive way.

8. What about telling family tales? In our experience, children love to hear stories about themselves. They can put up with the same old tale of things they did when they were tiny or listen to the recounting of family events from the past over and over again. It's the stuff of making history with them.

9. Think of a situation where your child bottled up their feelings. To help them get across what they were feeling, draw a simple picture about the occasion and add some speech bubbles to the picture. Then hunt for a few words that express what your child was feeling – you could look through magazines or a newspaper together and cut and paste them to the speech bubbles. Then talk it through with them.

All of these ideas are dependent on your child's age and developmental ability, of course, so adapt them to suit. And please make sure you don't get too carried away with doing exercises and not doing nice things for yourself. But if you really get into all this, there are some great books with exercises you can do with children of all ages and we've listed a few suggestions at the end of the book. It might help to know that (if you are in the mood) parents have told us they've quite enjoyed doing them.

Doing activities like these together is less about solving problems and more about helping your child to find ways to express parts of who they are. You're essentially helping them to get used to noticing their own thoughts and feelings and how these might impact on their behaviour. Encouraging your child to talk about their feelings is a really effective way to help them to get to know themselves. And optimistically speaking, if you've followed the ideas offered in this chapter and practised them repeatedly, even though you might be exhausted and have no social life by now, your children will be some distance on the way to developing a good sense of who are they are.

If this is the case, you can now go on to thinking about how they might change some things about themselves. And even if it's not the case yet, you can dip into this section anyway because, you never know, something just might help.

But he doesn't want to change, he's stuck in his misery, always saying he's useless.

First off, we asked parents what they did to motivate their children and young people to consider the possibility of change. Here's a few of their ideas:

- Listen well and check that you really understand what they mean.

- Ask them how they would like to be.

- Ask them about their hopes and what they want to happen in the future.

- Ask them what might stop them reaching their goals.

- Do a pros and cons list with them to find out whether making changes or staying as things are feels best.

- Ask them questions in a curious sort of way so they ponder about themselves.

- Ask them who they'd like to be and why.

- Remind them of changes they or other people have made for the better, even though they or others thought they wouldn't.

This list is a general collection of ideas, all worth trying. But what if your child doesn't like what they see? For example, imagine the child who has an inner belief that they're useless and can't do anything right. Even though they have all the basics in place or are coping well with school, for example, it's likely that they'll find it doubly difficult to believe they can accomplish a new task or make new friends because it just doesn't fit with their inner belief of being 'useless'. Helping a child like this to change the way they think about things would be a very resilient move on your part. This is potentially very tricky territory, one, because the beliefs children have about themselves shape their lives and, two, because it's very hard to do.

It might help to remember that personality is made up of two things: temperament, which is biological and genetic, and character, which develops out of early experience. All of us have aspects of our personalities which we might not like, give us grief from time to time and predispose us to certain tendencies. Some children are born with unappealing temperaments that we may not be able to change much. However, the great news is that character can be formed. So our actions and words can have a huge effect on children's self-esteem and the way they perceive themselves in the world.

For example, teaching children to think positively isn't always easy especially if they've got into bad habits. We're thinking here of those children who frequently only notice the negatives, or blow things out of proportion, minimize their achievements or jump to extreme conclusions. To help children think in more helpful and positive ways, we suggest breaking things down into smaller steps. Have a look at the 'Step by Step' exercise on the next page.

For kids who are really stuck, and see a catastrophe around every corner, you could try a well-known psychological technique involving them setting up their own experiment.

STEP BY STEP

Step 1

Start out by asking your child to spot the unhelpful ways they think about things when they feel stressed or disappointed about something. You might have to offer a few prompts or suggestions from what you have observed at this point. Try and get them to be specific; for example: 'He doesn't want to be my friend. Nobody likes me', or 'I can't find my coat, it must have been stolen, it's not safe here.'

Step 2

Ask them to catch themselves when they think in these ways by writing it down or recording it somehow.

Step 3

Ask them to think of alternative ways of thinking about the incident. Write these ideas down with or for them.

Step 4

See if they will also practise using the alternative way of thinking out loud, next time something difficult or disappointing happens.

Step 5

Ask them what it feels like to think about it differently.

Step 6

Encourage them to keep on trying because, like any habit, we have to practise the new way to drown out the old.

Changing habits can be really tough, so if you're not getting anywhere don't forget that it can make sense to move on and concentrate on a different RT potion because approaching things from a different angle can shift things sometimes. So now let's go on to helping children relate better to other people. Have a go at the 'We're Conducting an Experiment' exercise on the next page.

WE'RE CONDUCTING AN EXPERIMENT

1. Ask your child to think of something that they think is going to not work out for them.

    Example: At school I'm going to be shouted at all day.

2. Get them to give it a score out of 10 or a percentage as to how badly it will go (if your child can't do numbers at all, get them to colour in the number of squares out of 10, on a piece of paper).

    Example: At school there's a 100% chance I'll be shouted at all day.

3. They go to school, and when they come back, ask what percentage they were shouted at. Chances are they'll notice that it's less than they thought. If they don't, though, you get them to work through everything that happened in the day with you, and help them to see the moments when they weren't shouted at. This will help them alter their perception.

Note: If the experiment reveals that they are thinking really negatively, you may have to remind them that it's normal to have their positive feelings go up and down depending on what might be happening in their lives. Get them to try the experiment on different days. It helps them appreciate that just because they're feeling glum one day doesn't mean they won't be feeling excited on another.

Teaching children to understand other people's feelings

Researchers specializing in child development have found that the ability for children to tune into other people's feelings is really important for them being happy in life. It helps them to get along and to feel welcome in the wider world. So it's not enough to just help children to feel good about themselves – this has to translate to learning to care about others, and to feel confident and happy in company. But the way children understand other people's feelings is to some extent a bit chicken and egg. Much of the research on attachment, which we've mentioned in Chapter 2, Belonging, suggests that kids learn to understand other people's feelings only through having had their own feelings properly understood and responded to, which is why we've included so much on ways to help children talk about their feelings.

When you think about it, giving priority to helping children to understand other people's feelings is quite obvious. Not many of us like really selfish people who never, ever think about what other people want or need. But first, children need to be able to read and understand other people's feelings to then know something about how to be in social situations with them. We can't stress this point too much. This might not be something you want to hear, because it might not be an area that you find that easy to manage, or maybe it's not something you value as an important life skill yourself. Furthermore, it can be particularly difficult for children with complex needs, and so it might well be an area you'll have to work doubly hard on. But just because it's difficult and you might only get so far with it doesn't mean you take it off the list.

> My son has autistic spectrum disorder (ASD). And I don't want to set myself up with the task of making him understand how people feel because some ASD children may never have the capacity for that.

Let's face it, some of the habits of kids with complex needs mean they don't readily endear themselves to others. Not helping them to learn to read the signals more accurately means they are in danger of putting people off and really struggling to have friends. Even if you know in your heart of hearts that reading feelings is never going to be their strong point, it's still worth hanging on to the idea we introduced in the Coping chapter, 'Fake it till you make it', because, you never know, they might just get it. Acting in the world as if they do, so people will be nicer to them, and not mind being around your family so much, is worth the effort. Okay, so let's take the plunge. Break it down a bit, hang onto your sense of hope and try hard to notice the smaller achievements.

What about trying out the tried and tested idea of 'smiley faces'? This involves having a copied sheet of faces, all with different expressions that you then use as a prompt to help children link expressions with feelings.

It's a good thing to start with because it suggests to the child that there are a lot of fine distinctions and subtleties around the face that you have to learn to read. And it's a fun way to help them begin to notice what other people might be feeling as well as recognizing their own

feelings. But it doesn't have to mean always getting your exercise book out. Take the chance to use ordinary everyday events to practise.

> Every morning before we go out to school, while we're putting our shoes on, I say I'm that face, he says he's that face, and his brother goes I'm that face…or I'm all of them…it's just getting into the habit of him going 'I feel' because one of the things he has a big issue about is feelings. He has no understanding of other people's and finds it really hard with his own – so you begin to get into the habit of feeling something and doing something – not just expressions, it's tone of voice, body language.

Or ask them to think of famous people they like and talk about what it must be like to be them. What their days would be like, where they would live, what they would like to eat and wear, what they would feel like if this happened and so on.

> I use the characters he plays with on the computer games before I get onto real people. I say over his shoulder, 'Look, when he swipes the sword and he looks like that, he's scared.'

It may be that for your children it's best not to talk so much about what they feel, but look for opportunities to encourage them to put themselves in the other person's shoes. For example, using stories and play figures to construct situations where something good or bad happens can be a great way to explore what a child thinks the characters have felt in the situation. It's also a chance to learn about how to be sociable because you can get the characters to talk with each other and exchange thoughts and ideas.

> When he was being a right pain at the table in the cafe for example, I'd pretend his fingers were puppies and talked to them…oh what's he going to do, or he's not eating his dinner.

Or you might start by helping them to develop an awareness of how their behaviours affect other people. Ask them to talk you through something that they did that really made someone else feel good, for example. Or something they did that made someone feel worried.

Rather than just relying on words, if your child doesn't like talking about these things, you could try getting them to draw a picture, or write it down, or act it out. Anything that helps get that awareness going. It may be that you could enlist another child or adult to help you if it's really looking like you're getting nowhere with this one very fast.

Encouraging children to treat themselves how everyone likes to be treated might be another way in. For example, some children like to have their own space. Having somewhere to go on their own without other people around can help them notice their own needs, which in turn might help them to imagine what other people need. When we asked a small group of children whether they had space in their house for themselves they were all able to talk about how important it was to them. Without any prompting, they said it was a place where they went to calm down, to let off steam, to do their own thing. So maybe helping children to learn to be with their own company could be a way in to their appreciating that others also need their own space.

And the same applies to you too. Taking yourself out on your own date and doing things alone not only offers the chance of new experiences but you also get the opportunity to focus inwards. If you're always with someone else chances are you're constantly paying attention to how they are or what they are feeling and not yourself.

As we've already said, one of the advantages of learning about how others feel is that you can begin to read social situations and adapt your own behaviour accordingly. We probably all know that if we enter a room of children and adults all shouting at each other, we can make a guess that people are angry and that we might need to tread carefully so as not to put our foot in it. Lots of children don't always know how to read these kinds of situations. It's a difficulty parents come back to time and time again.

And it's possible that children and young people with complex needs will also be dealing with a greater incidence of unwelcoming or excluding behaviour from those around them than other children. Any tips for getting on well with others should be stored away in your memory ready for use at a moment's notice because parents tell us that it can take some time for their children to make progress in this area.

Basic politeness and social niceties are important here. This probably sounds ever so obvious but it can take a bit of practice to teach children these skills, and it's tempting to give up on it. But knowing how to start a conversation, keep it going and ending one are skills most of us probably take for granted. Basic reminders to children about how to behave, not interrupting, not swearing, making eye contact, taking turns, role modelling good social skills yourself and helping them to develop a stock of useful phrases to use in social situations is also worth doing. We mentioned this in the Coping chapter too.

> I make sure my kids always ask me how I am when they see me and I ask them. They probably don't really care, but they say it like rote, and then when they meet other people they say it too. Other people really notice that my kids are polite and friendly and forgive them a lot because of it.

Another useful strategy can be to involve them in volunteering, helping others and linking up with community projects. These situations require children to care for others. Looking after a pet, having the job of taking the school register to the office and having specific tasks in the house are all opportunities worth using to build a sense of personal responsibility, which we mention next. Research on happiness by Richard Layard (2005) and others shows that children who think about other people, and have regular concrete experience of helping others, really do better in life and are happier. Take note though; for some of you getting this to happen will be quite a challenge. A child is usually quite self-centred and only able to begin to think about how it is for others after they've reached their sixth or seventh birthday. For children with developmental and other difficulties, this will be even more of a challenge.

The noble truth of enlisting is probably even more crucial when thinking of ways to teach a child to understand others. You could use those people already involved in your child's life to help with this one. Working with and through those who know your child best and are likely to be around for a while makes sense. You might even be able to use school counsellors or learning mentors if they are on offer, although we realize that school may not be the most positive place for your child. You may want to pull in the help of extended family members even if only for the smallest of inputs.

Essentially, what we are saying here is that if your child can recognize their own feelings, and understand others', you're on to a winner. What follows on from this is to help them take responsibility for themselves, because if they do that there is more chance that they will change behaviours that aren't helpful to them.

Helping children to take responsibility for themselves

You want your children to take responsibility for the things they do that are good – you want them to take the credit. But you also want them to take responsibility for the things they do that cause something that's not quite so positive – like hurting another's feelings or breaking something.

This remedy is about how we might encourage children to build their capacity to take responsibility for themselves. It builds on knowing themselves. It's about helping them to see that they have a relationship to the things and the people around them that they can impact on, rather than assuming things happen to them all the time.

There's a very strong link between learning to take responsibility for yourself and coming to know your own sense of usefulness and personal power. Grabbing hold of daily opportunities to help children to experience some control over situations and understand they have the power to make choices and decisions in their life is a good way into sowing the idea that they can impact their lives rather than life happening to them.

If I do it this way rather than that way, it might make a difference and I'll feel better about it.

Learning about the consequences of decisions – that's what I want him to learn. So he knows he doesn't just have to react but he can make choices about how he responds.

Obviously, you have to take account of your child's difficulties when thinking about how much it's reasonable to expect them to be able to take responsibility for themselves. You need to set realistic goals that fit with their ability to direct their responses or shape their own worlds. But be careful about assuming they can't step up to this challenge.

It's a reason that things are harder, it's not an excuse for opting out.

The danger, of course, with this potion is that we can end up yelling and getting ourselves down because shifts are slow in arriving, or we get to thinking our children are deliberately avoiding taking responsibility for their actions or we feel exasperated because they just don't seem able to tolerate their achievements.

Our suggestion is to pick just a few things to concentrate on and avoid doing too much all at once. For those children who struggle to be proud of things they have done well, you might want to try one of these ideas:

Taking responsibility for the good things

- Get your child to list three things they are proud of and put these on a card. Encourage them to practise reading or saying these things when they go to bed at night and when they wake up in the morning, and even better if they can say them out loud.

- Encourage situations where children can put their own stamp on things.

- Introduce the idea of a 'worries box'. Some children respond well to having a safe container for difficult feelings: 'Shall we put that one away on the shelf in the worries box for now?'

And for those children who find it hard to manage and regulate their trickier feelings and reduce their problem behaviours, we think it really helps to side-step blame – with the following caveat. Sometimes you have to speak bluntly. You have to say that hitting you or their brothers and sisters is abusive, that stealing is immoral, that swearing and calling you names is cruel. Children will sense that you are taking charge. Children who act this way are not usually in control of themselves, even though it seems as though they are. While they may get a quick buzz from lashing out, it can keep their deepest fears alive – that they are uncontrollable and that you can't calm them down.

> I tend to think of cause and effect because it's more neutral than consequences and blame. It gives me a level playing field in which to discuss things and a different way of dealing with things that go wrong. This is the cause, this is what happened, this is the effect, how do we do that now, is that good, is that bad, is it an effect we wanted, how do we negotiate that... I find it keeps blame out of the picture.

Taking responsibility for the not so good things

If you want a child to change their behaviour sometimes you first have to accept the feelings they have, show you can tolerate them and find ways to deal with them, together. You might find one of these ideas helpful:

1. Name without shaming. Sometimes children need to have their emotions named because they cannot recognize them when they are in a heightened state. Explain that anger is a feeling like any other and is okay. While it might be understandable that they express it by being violent or aggressive, it's not acceptable. Help your child to practise alternative ways of managing their rage or panic like doing some fast exercise or punching pillows.

2. If it's hard for your child to use words to explain their feelings, get into the habit of using images or use things like how a feeling might sound, look or smell.

3. Help them to anticipate any triggers so they can make decisions about how to respond to these as early as possible.

4. When things flare up, keep the tone of your voice calm and use strong, grounded body language so your child knows you can keep things safe and contained. 'Fake it till you make it' might come in handy here!

5. Don't find excuses for unacceptable behaviour. You want to help them to understand the social consequences of being aggressive. For example, remind them they have to pay for any damage by making them clear up the mess, docking their pocket money or giving them extra jobs.

We can't prevent our children from experiencing uncomfortable feelings and we all make mistakes. But what we do, or did in the past, is not who we are and children may need to be reminded of this from time to time. Instilling a sense of moral decency and an understanding of right and wrong can take ages with our kids, because it's only as children mature that they begin to feel embarrassment and to care about what others think.

> My child has a lot of imaginary friends – she chats to them and tells them off, she says things like, 'That's really mean, you can't do that', and I join in sometimes, as a way of trying to teach her what's right.

Helping children to become independent is also about helping them learn to take responsibility for themselves.

> Every morning before he takes his medication, he can't sit still. We all know he's hyperactive so either we pander to the hyperactivity, or we say we need to learn how to sit still – because for me it's more important that he learns that in a classroom or working environment that he has to sit down, even though it is incredibly hard for him. So it's about teaching him to manage that for himself – to keep his bottom on the chair for five minutes. It's a first step to learning how to take responsibility for himself.

And just before we finish, are you taking responsibility for your own feelings? You can make choices and decisions too about how much to worry and fret about your children. We've really promoted the idea of you and your child working on taking responsibility together. Make sure you have someone to share your experiences with or a space to manage your own feelings about what's going on. It's not worth going it alone.

> I *can* do something to take my mind off my kids, it's in my own hands.

Fostering children's talents

The place to start with this one is to find out what really matters to your children. What do they most admire in others? What would they most like to be praised for? How do they like to be praised? Because once we've explored this a little, then we'll have some idea of how we might support them to make these things happen.

Fostering talents is about building up a child's resources, and a well-resourced child has more to call on to help them find their feet when things get tough. By fostering children's talents, we give them the chance to understand more about their abilities and it's particularly important for those children who are being left out too often by their peers. Let's face it, many of the children we are mindful of are excluded from school, don't get invited to as many parties or sleep-overs and have trouble finding after-school activities and clubs that welcome them with open arms. We know that when children don't have a lot of these things in their life, what they do have has added significance. So the few friends and talents they do have matter more than they might to someone with lots of friends and loads of abilities and masses of things going on.

Some parents say their children have had such horrible experiences going to clubs, or being excluded from things they enjoy but can't manage quite as well as others, that they want to retreat and build a secure base first and then think of new opportunities to try out. They're cautious about exposing their kids to more hurt, so we appreciate that striking a balance between protecting your children from disappointment and exposing them to risk can be tricky. But children need normal ordinary experiences.

Fostering children's talents is about building on the qualities and good points they already have and maximizing their influence. Often children are good at things that they or we don't notice or they don't value. So hunting for their abilities, sensitivities or talents is about bringing their social capital or their 'street cred' out for others to see. Sometimes, just one of these things can make all the difference.

> He's really good at taking other people's feelings into account. But he goes overboard. If he wins a prize at school he has to give it to someone else.

Capturing the talent and directing it well is the task at hand here. It's a bit different to fostering their interests mentioned in Chapter 4, Coping. This remedy is more about being on the look out for any flair, gift or ability a child has – that might be buried – but that when unearthed can be exploited to their advantage. A little success can go such a long way for our children. Here are a few ideas for grabbing hold of talents.

1. Catch your child being successful – when they do well, notice it and praise it. If it's something they can do again, get them to repeat it for you or show other family members.

   > I keep a 'Well done' book for him and for me.

2. When your child says 'I'm no good at…, I'm useless', remind them how much better they are than before.

3. Learning to describe what you want rather than what you don't want can take a bit of practice but it's worth it because positive messages breed hope.

   > I knew he was managing to use a spoon at school so I stopped saying 'Don't eat with your hands' and instead said, 'I hear you're really good at using a spoon. I'll find that special spoon I've got for you to use at home.'

4. Having your child's talents on the tip of your tongue to use at a moment's notice can really help when they've had a bad day, are feeling a bit lousy or can't do something. What would your list include?

> See, you don't need me to help, you've got that bit of homework out of the way, tomorrow you can have a bit of play time.

We guess we might be sounding a bit naive to those of you who've tried to encourage all sorts of activities and interests without much success. Approach this remedy with a spirit of adventure rather than sheer desperation, as it's true that you might have as many failures as successes. But doing fun stuff and fostering talents is a way to begin to experience some choice in life, some sense of achievement and competence.

> I just couldn't bear having another conversation about the computer game. I was slowly going mad. So I decided to try to think of the things that we both like doing. I had to dig deep but I found one...

Using tried and tested treatments for specific problems

This remedy is included because sometimes no matter what we do and how hard we try to support children with complex needs – by instilling hope, helping them to understand themselves and others, learning to take responsibility or fostering talents – it can make sense to use tried and tested treatments, that engage with their Core Self, as well.

> I thought perhaps I should just take a chill pill and challenge my own beliefs. Perhaps medication might work for my child. We'd tried so much, putting in a major effort. Maybe, just maybe, he was born that way, and a couple of pills every day might make him feel better and be easier to live with. And yet, even as I say this, I feel shocked at what I'm thinking.

Essentially we mean exploring the possible benefits of medication and therapies that directly, and often swiftly, change something fundamental. But it also means taking note that many of the ideas we've offered throughout this book, within the other RT potions – Basics, Belonging, Learning and Coping – have been shown to work time and time again. Actually, this whole book includes tried and tested stuff that we've researched, used ourselves or discovered helps by asking other parents. The difference between these and what we mean by tried and tested treatments for specific problems is that here we are assuming that something needs more urgent attention or can be momentarily and even permanently fixed. This is controversial, but sometimes a treatment can really work where all else fails.

So even though you may feel reluctant to agree trying things out it seems sensible to us not to dismiss suggestions outright. Clearly, people have strong views about some treatments but do your own research. Parents have told us that recognizing the clear symptoms, behaviours and difficulties that come with a particular diagnosis or condition has really helped them to know what to do. It's given them a starting place from which to begin to research possible remedies, interventions and treatments. Find out what others think of the ideas, ask other parents or young people about their experiences of using different medications and treatments, enquire and delve a little.

The point we are making is that if you know a child is just intrinsically a certain way, they might just need something else to help them with that, and that's the way it is. So what's been tried and tested and works well to build a good Core Self?

Where are these treatments? Give them to me now!

As you might have guessed, we cannot provide much detail because every child is different and unique. For example, think about the children with disruptive behaviour disorders, who are non-compliant, hostile, aggressive or hyperactive. We're thinking here of children with a diagnosis of Attention-Deficit Hyperactivity Disorder (ADHD) or Oppositional Conduct Disorder (OCD) who have trouble sitting still or lash out unexpectedly. Many are prescribed drugs, for example Ritalin, to help manage their symptoms. While we're aware of the controversy and the strongly held views about using medication, lots of parents and professionals back up its use to help children to sit still so they can manage to learn something in class. And when used as part of a larger package of support that includes parent training and behavioural therapy there is convincing evidence that suggests it's worth trying. But what the medication and its dosage is, and what's included in the behaviour therapy and parent training programmes, might be very different for each child. Which takes us back to our original point – do your own research, ask questions and delve a little before you make your decision.

My child and I had family therapy, school counselling, behaviour plans, then we tried diet but in the end the thing that worked best was Ritalin for us. It was good we did the other stuff, because it helps with his ADHD, but we could see that it was never going to be enough. In his case, the drugs helped, because we couldn't do any more than we were doing.

It can be really hard trying to find out what the evidence is for certain treatments. When we did our research for this remedy, we found that some evidence was very convincing while other reports were more open about the uncertainty that can exist about how best to treat certain problems. For example, there doesn't appear to be any ideal drug treatment for children with Tourette's syndrome, but there are some medications that help and the research into individual behavioural approaches and parent training looks promising. Using anti-depressant medication for children with anxiety disorders has been shown to be effective but not all children improve with medication. Behavioural techniques can be effective for treatment of phobias but it's important not to lump all these techniques and therapies together because it appears there are aspects of different programmes that work better for different difficulties. While there is less research available on the effectiveness of systemic or psychodynamic psychotherapies, this doesn't mean they don't work, it just means there isn't enough research as yet to definitely help us know if it's worth the effort. And some of the research is with teenagers so it's not easy to know if the findings are transferable to children.

What we're trying to say is that, where there is some knowledge that exists about a particular condition, try and integrate that knowledge into your own way of working to build Core Self. This is where drawing on some of the other ideas of Core Self needs to be linked together. First of all, it makes sense to keep hold of the idea of experimenting, trying things out. You might, for example, have tried something before and it didn't work but this may have been because your child was too young, the conditions weren't right or it wasn't possible to be consistent. So you need to catch hold of your sense of hope again.

I just couldn't put any more effort into flogging a dead horse.

Or you may want to think about how you explain the medication or treatment to your child so they begin to understand for themselves why they are trying it out. This could also include you explaining why you, as their parent, want them to try it out. Sometimes, children can take on the challenge of trying new things when they have the information that helps make sense of the 'experiment'. It's another way to model them taking responsibility. And while they're in this trial stage, think about focusing on fostering their talents, so they have a sense of their ability to go the distance. Keep in mind what the philosopher and doctor Hippocrates said: 'The natural healing force within each one of us is the greatest force in getting well.'

And not only can you draw on some of the other ideas of Core Self, you can link this potion with the other RT potions. Let's illustrate what we mean. For children who are clinically depressed, it's highly likely that their mood can be improved with medication, particularly if the features of their depression include sleeping problems, loss of appetite and decreased physical activity. But alongside using medication there are extra things you can draw on from the other RT potions to help. When anyone's depressed they are likely to slow down because they have less enthusiasm and motivation. Children can tend to want to stay in bed all day and avoid going to school. But using the ideas of exercise and fresh air from the Basics potion can direct their attention away from themselves. Some research even suggests that physical activity is just as effective as medication. Doing things and getting children out and about can help them to shift their feelings of hopelessness. Simple things that uplift them and give them a sense of joy, like laughing and singing, can help too. Having that song they know the words to playing loudly or making sure they watch that TV programme they think is funny are easy things to include in daily life. Or drawing on the ideas within the potion of Belonging can also be significant. Ideally children need a number of people to support them when they feel this vulnerable. So while we know from research that people who have someone they trust and can confide in are the least likely to become depressed, you cannot do this alone. You and they need to call on your network of friends to help.

And, remember, even when things like medication can't directly treat a condition, it may be helpful in the short or medium-term management of problems. If you haven't slept for months and you're losing the ability to take care of yourself and your child, using medication to help them to sleep for a short while, so that you can catch up, may be the best thing to do on balance. Using tried and tested treatments is about the things that can be done to help boost the other things we do to build a child's resilience.

The Omega 3 fish oils seem to have made a real difference to his concentration: school have commented on it. Apparently you have to take it for at least a couple of months or more to see any benefit. It's expensive so luckily another parent told me about getting it pre-scribed by the GP.

Sometimes you might just want to try things out – as long as you do it for long enough to judge whether you and your child get any benefit – and have some guidance about the best way of stopping. So if you are feeling sceptical, our message from this section is to just consider trying something different. There really are situations where tried and tested remedies can make all the difference, and remember, you might only need them for a short while.

Conclusion

We hope we've begun to illustrate how there are mechanisms at work that come from *within* the individual child that are also worth paying attention to. These mechanisms are less connected with what happens on the outside and more to do with what happens on the inside.

The thought patterns that children learn are often set very early in their lives and they frequently have trouble making sense of them. Our job is to help them to decipher their thoughts so they can begin to build more resilient core beliefs and ideas about themselves and their worlds. As parents and professionals working with children, we have the chance to actively promote their journey towards greater self-awareness, self-esteem and confidence.

I think self-esteem is the basis of RT.

We mentioned in the introduction to this book that things like good looks and intelligence are often present in children who do well in the face of major difficulties. And we've played these down because we thought that as there is relatively little that can be done to alter these givens, it was better to concentrate on what can be done. You might think that altering a child's inner view about themselves is also pretty hard to shift, especially when the resilience literature suggests that, irrespective of a child's situation or the influences from outside, they hold inner views and beliefs about themselves.

However, by encouraging children to understand themselves, others and their own part in shaping their lives, we *can* help them to discover new meanings and new beliefs about themselves. It's also a really good basis for helping children discover which parts of themselves they'd like to change – if they don't know themselves, how could they imagine how they might want to be different?

Core Self offers us some pointers for ways of going about this most important of tasks and, while we have said that working at this deeper individual level takes time and requires quite a lot of patience on our part, we are suggesting that approaching it like learning a new language might help. This time, it's not French or Chinese, but a new emotional language.

We suppose that it won't have come as any surprise to you that we think it makes sense to examine our own Core Self in order to build it in children. Having an understanding of our sense of worth, our own beliefs about ourself and our own abilities, can make us more able to recognize it in children and, in turn, help us to facilitate children understanding their own.

> Having to manage my depression has forced me to do that personal development stuff. I learnt that you've got to be aware of yourself first before you can accept yourself, then you can move forward to change the bits that you are not quite happy with in order to rebuild the sense of self and self-worth and hope.

While we've tried to offer a few practical suggestions to illustrate ways to help a child to feel good about themselves, most of Core Self work is about how we approach the task. All of the ideas suggested in Core Self involve a way of being. And each of the characteristics – instilling a sense of hope; teaching children to understand other people's feelings and getting to know themselves; helping children to take responsibility for themselves; and fostering their talents and using tried and tested treatments for specific problems – are interconnected. Concentrating on just one will have a positive knock-on effect on the others.

Even though you might be struggling with your own issues about your self-worth or your effectiveness, don't be too hard on yourself. Of course it's much easier to assist children with low self-esteem when you already have a healthy sense of it yourself, but even if this is fragile, the two can be nurtured alongside each other. It's simply about focusing on the ordinary, little things we can do as part of their regular lives, to build their internal personal strengths.

Imagine getting to the point where the children we care about can take quiet pleasure in being themselves. Magic!

Let's recap

Core Self – the potion works very deeply to shape a child's character.

- Instil a sense of hope.

- Help the child to know her/himself.

- Teach the child to understand other people's feelings.

- Help child take responsibility for her/himself.

- Foster their talents.

- There are tried and tested treatments for specific problems; use them.

CHAPTER 6

LET'S GET REAL: IT'S TOUGH BUT SO ARE YOU

Introduction

Well, you've persevered and got to the end of our introduction to Resilient Therapy. Assuming we've made ourselves clear, you now know something about what we mean by the four noble truths that underpin this approach:

Resilient Therapy's noble truths

1. Acceptance

2. Conservation

3. Commitment

4. Enlisting

And you're more familiar with the five 'magic' potions that suggest remedies for you to try:

Resilient Therapy's magic potions

1. Basics
2. Belonging
3. Learning
4. Coping
5. Core Self

We're really hoping you're now applying some part of RT to your own situations. If you're not quite there yet, have a go at the 'Bringing RT into your Life' exercise over the page. (You still might find it useful, even if you've now become an RT bore.)

We're sure RT can offer you something, and if we sound too cocky, here's why. First, it's based on sound resilience research; second, it's been developed alongside help from parents and professionals with experience of raising and supporting children with complex needs; and third, we're using it effectively in our own homes and in our work with other children and their families.

Right from the start, RT was designed with disadvantaged children in mind. Some of the books we've read around this subject seem to have been written for ordinary children and families and not the complex children and situations you're dealing with. So our intention has been to try to ground this book in the real world of bringing up children with complex needs. When we've done workshops and presentations, we've received some very encouraging feedback from both parents and professionals.

> I find it difficult to look at things that are difficult – it's difficult talking about stuff that she finds difficult and that I find difficult, but RT makes it possible to do.

> It just really cheered me up – understanding what resilience really means and having a couple of tools and just having a few comforting words.

> It helped me re-find my sense of hope when I was sliding.

BRINGING RT INTO YOUR LIFE

Identify one tricky thing that you have experienced in your life (if only there had been just one!) that you have had to overcome:

How did you deal with this situation?

Now think about the five magic potions – there's an illustration of the 'Magic Box' and a table at the end of the introductory chapter.

Did any of the potions, or the remedies within them, help you deal with the situation?

If they did, you've got RT in your bones! If not, can you think now that you know more about resilience whether any would have been helpful?

If you've got any left-over energy, give it a go with your child in mind.

Identify one tricky thing that they have had to face and overcome.

How did they do it, or how did you help them?

Which of the magic potions and remedies, or what combination, helped them deal with it?

My attitude, my behaviour and my children's behaviour has really shifted. It feels like everything has clicked into place.

Others have been less enthusiastic. They've commented that 'it's just common sense', and 'it's not a real therapy'. We agree – on the whole. We want the RT potions to make sense to people. Lots of the remedies and ideas ought to be quite obvious and straightforward to understand. That's the easy bit. But try putting them into practice!

In our experience, applying these seemingly simple ideas is no small task. Angie knows this stuff inside out, and having spent hours hanging round her house co-writing this book, Kim thinks she has a really sunny approach to parenting. Even so, the demands of raising her three fabulous kids leaves her stumped more than she'd like. And Kim knows it's hard because she's seen how really competent parents still struggle with family life.

Although we might not be very popular saying this, but professionals and people outside the immediate family can seriously ignore or misunderstand the realities of 24/7 care. It's surprising how frequently problems get pointlessly located in children or their parents, they get referred from pillar to post, or miss out completely on timely specialist help. We think it truly helps when organizations and practitioners work hard to get their heads round what it might be like to live in such complex situations. Not so simple though!

RT is something you integrate with what you are already doing. It's not a prescriptive method that requires you to dump all that you've already learned and use instead. Nor is it a rigid formula that has to be applied in a certain way.

Calling RT a therapy has been quite controversial. Some people expect a much more formal approach for a therapy, and think anyone doing it should have a handful of diplomas and letters after their names, showing how well trained they are. Or they expect it to have a specific process with a start and an end. We've stuck with the term 'therapy', because we want to reclaim its original meaning. Derek, one of the authors of the first RT book, loves reading ancient philosophy and other learned works (he hasn't got a load of kids with complex needs at home demanding him to do RT quizzes all day). The original Greek meaning of therapy is 'healing force'. He's always going on to us about how the best healing is using the resources we already have – it's the basis of healing in orthopaedics for example – just put the support on and the bones will heal themselves. Whether you're healing yourself, or someone else is helping you, simply put, we reckon that's what RT is about.

You could think about it as a complex and multi-layered undertaking if you want to. We think it's better to think of RT as straightforward 'ordinary magic'. RT is essentially an attitude and an approach. It offers a series of ideas, remedies and techniques to use in everyday ways.

You can go through the ideas and it signposts you to what you can do. It's also a way of thinking about things – becoming a resilient therapist means making creative adjustments and strategic choices to suit your particular child and your particular circumstances. So while you might be concentrating on just one potion like Belonging and helping your child to make friends, for example, you'll also have in the back of your mind an awareness of how this might link with Coping or Core Self. Getting used to thinking, doing and tackling things resiliently, of course, is going to take practice.

Realistically speaking, RT needs to be incorporated into your routine ways of parenting, if it has any real chance of working for you and your children. That's why we think you have to get real about what's possible.

Getting real

We reckon you probably deserve a medal for even contemplating anything new in your life, so great that you've got this far with RT. For lots of our kids, disadvantage comes in many shapes and sizes, often all at the same time. Each individual problem can, and probably does, link up with others to create more complexities that are hard to unravel.

Repetition, consistency, reliability, ongoing regularity, pace…tired already?

And all this while you're trying to get on with day-to-day life! Parents remind us, and Angie knows from first-hand experience, that it's tricky when you've got other kids around. Siblings can feel left out when their brother or sister is getting all the attention because their difficulty demands it. It's hard to split yourself and deal with one child kicking off, for example, while the other one needs a reassuring hug.

The unpredictability of his behaviour was not something I wanted them to witness – they were so young, but there wasn't much I could do about it.

Different children often need different things from us at the same time. Homework helper, cook and bottle washer, feeder and carer, partner, friend, resilience builder too! And, as Kim remembers, sleepless nights seeing to children's needs and lone parenting make the challenges even harder. You know you're tired when you wake up in the night to go to the toilet, and you have to say, 'Come on leg, we can do this.'

Our lives might not always be turning out quite as we imagined, but it is what we've got.

> Sometimes I go to bed thinking I hate my life, but things will look better in the morning. Awful though it all is, you've gotta laugh, and you do feel better after a decent night's sleep.

> I don't know when or why it suddenly dawned on me that there had to be something better than this. The conditions of my birth and my geography suggested I'd just plod along like everyone else around me, but I just knew if I took some responsibility for my future, it could be better.

Getting the balance right

We have a choice about how we relate to our circumstances – we can make ourselves miserable or we can make ourselves strong. Of course, sometimes you have to give yourself permission to let everything fall apart even when it really goes against the grain for you. Feeling miserable can humble us and soften our hearts so that we better understand how it is for others. It can also give us time to grieve, if we have to.

But you don't want to make this your norm; being constantly miserable doesn't get you very far, and it's not very nice for children to be around. So what if you are really worn down by it all most of the time? Or get so inside a problem that you lose focus and get confused about what you want, or what you think needs to happen next? Well, stand back for a moment. And then, even if you can make a bit of an effort on a good day but don't feel like you can do much more, it's worth trying to apply at least a few of the RT ideas. Parents say it can work for them too. But it won't be easy all of the time – no surprises there!

Trying out some of the RT ideas might not be very familiar to you or your characteristic way of doing things, so don't too be too hard on yourself. Just give it a go and see what happens.

> RT has given me much more of an insight into me and I thought it was going to be all about him and it hasn't at all been all about him. It's been about my attitude to him and my attitude to myself as well.

Our guess is that we all have doubts and uncertainties at times about what's realistic to expect of our kids. On the one hand, assuming loads and reaching for the stars can leave us coming down to earth with a thud. While on the other hand, wrapping our kids in cotton wool and thinking they can't learn anything new isn't helpful either. It's often like walking a tightrope trying to get the right balance between accepting our children and their limitations whilst also challenging them to try harder.

A certain amount of fluctuation in your confidence and how good you feel about your ability to use the RT potions and remedies is quite natural. No one needs you to be perfect. Give yourself a break. Lighten up and relax. We're all only here on this earth for a short while. You cannot single-handedly create a child who manages life's challenges resiliently overnight.

> One of my greatest survival skills is seeing the funny side, or taking a long-term view, of what my child does, even in the moment. It's an art, but you can learn it.

Giving RT a go

If it's making their lives work in more resilient ways you're after, we think one of the best ways of building resilience in your children is to model it yourself. RT might just help you to develop the skills you need to give your kids the best chance of managing their lives more resiliently.

But even if you're feeling a tad doubtful or unsure about whether in times of stress RT will quite cut the mustard, we hope you will at least give it a go. Do yourself a favour – when starting out, try it when things are not so frantic.

And look after yourself in the process. Get into a routine of giving yourself a little bit of quiet time in the mornings – some of us old hippies call this 'mindfully creating your day'. Each morning when you wake up lie still for a few moments – maybe use your breathing to ground you in the moment – in other words, breathe deeply and notice your breath. Actively picture the day you want and the qualities you wish to bring to it – for example, resilience! Or better still break it down into whatever potion or remedy you're focusing on. Getting into doing this can help you start your day well and get you into a resilient mindset. Make it a habit. And however enthusiastic you get about RT, it's always important to take some time out for yourself.

> I have a regular babysitter; even when I don't feel like going out, the babysitter turns up anyway. I plan a couple of hours away and some-times I walk out the door and I don't know what I'm going to do.

Somehow it builds my resilience because someone else does the routine with my boys.

Here are a few reminders to help you get into the swing.

Top tips for giving RT a go

- **Practice**
  Practise being creative. Start out small and try just one thing at a time. Strike a balance between taking the risk to give a new idea a go and choosing something that is reasonably achievable. This way you are more likely to have some success which can often encourage us to keep on trying.

- **Experiment**
  Your child won't know whether or not you feel confident about what you're doing, so pretend you are! This allows you to test out new ideas and possibilities even though you're unsure about the outcome. Remember, RT can't do any damage.

- **Expect the unexpected**
  If you want something to change then be specific, but also remain open to new opportunities, new information and things going a little slower (or quicker) than you might have hoped.

- **Change your focus**
  Aim to have a few ideas and strategies up your sleeve. This takes the pressure off you if you're not feeling up to the original plan. It gives you other options to try out if necessary.

- **Pick your moments**
  Decide the best time to give your new idea a go – think about when it's likely to suit your child, and you, the best.

- **Listen to your children**
  No matter how old your child is, you have to work at their pace. Use your child's response to help you but, remember, sometimes things get worse before they get better especially if it's annoying behaviour you're working on. It can often be important they understand what you're doing too, as it's their chance to learn what you're teaching and encouraging.

- **Take it easy on yourself**
  It's reasonable given the nature of what you're doing, and the huge but different demands made of parents and professionals, to build in breaks, rewards and incentives. Looking after yourself helps to hold the resilient approach in mind.

- **Notice the little things**
  Take time to think about the little shifts and achievements. In the context of parenting children with complex needs, they might be huge. Change can come so slowly that it's actually a real skill to notice it. Or it may be that something hasn't got worse, when it might have done if you hadn't stepped in.

REFERENCES

Amaze (2008) *Tips for Claiming Disability Living Allowance.* Factsheet. Available at www.amazebrighton.org.uk/content_files/files/4_claiming_DLA.pdf, accessed 10 November 2008.

Amaze (2008) *Childcare Questions.* Factsheet. Available at www.amazebrighton.org.uk/content_files/files/7_childcare_questions.pdf, accessed 10 November 2008.

Amaze (2008) *Leisure.* Factsheet. Available at www.amazebrighton.org.uk/content_files/files/6_leisure.pdf, accessed 10 November 2008

Avery, D. (1999) 'Talking Tragedy – Identity Issues in the Parental Story of Disability.' In M. Corker and S. French (eds) *Disability Discourses.* Buckingham: Open University Press.

Barnes, M. *et al.* (2002) *Families and Children in Britain: Findings from the 2002 Families and Children Study (FACS).* DWP Research Report No. 206. CDS: Leeds.

Batten, A. (2006) *Make School Make Sense: Autism and Education, the Reality for Families Today.* London: NAS.

Birch, L.L. (1982) 'I don't like it; I never tried it: Effects of exposure on two-year-old children's food preferences.' *Appetite 3,* 4, 353–360.

Buckner, L. and Yeandle, S. (2006) *Managing More than Most.* London: Carers UK. Available at www.carersuk.org/Policyandpractice/Research/Employmentandcaring/1207231064, accessed 1 September 2008.

ChildWise (2007) *Monitor Trends Report 2007.* Norwich: ChildWise. Available at www.childwise.co.uk, accessed 1 September 2008.

Cole, M. and Cole, S.R. (1989) *The Development of Children.* New York: W.H. Freeman and Co.

DCSF (Department for Children, Schools and Families) (2008) *Permanent and Fixed Period Exclusions from Schools in England 2006/07.* Available at www.dcsf.gov.uk/rsgateway/DB/SFR/s000793/index.shtml, accessed 1 September 2008.

Department of Health (2004) *Summary of Intelligence on Physical Activity.* Available at www.yorkshireuniversities.ac.uk/docs/TPHN/YHPHPP/Summaries%20Pack/Physical%20Activity.pdf, accessed 10 November 2008.

Department of Health (2005) *At Least Five a Week: Evidence on the Impact of Physical Activity and its Relationship to Health. A Report from the Chief Medical Officer.* London: Department of Health.

Disability Rights Commission (2003) *Young Disabled People: A Survey of the Views and Experiences of Young Disabled People in Great Britain.* London: DRC.

Dobson, B. and Middleton, S. (1998) *Paying to Care: The Costs of Childhood Disability.* York: Joseph Rowntree Foundation.

EDCM (2007) *Disabled Children and Child Poverty. Briefing Paper by Every Disabled Child Matters Campaign.* Available at www.edcm.org.uk/pdfs/disabled_children_and_child_poverty.pdf, accessed 1 September 2008.

Expert Group on Hydration (2006) *Drinking in Schools.* Available at www.experthydration.com, accessed 1 September 2008.

Finch, N., Lawton, D., Williams, J. and Sloper, P. (2001) *Young Disabled People and Transport: Understanding their Needs and Requirements.* London: Department for Transport's Mobility and Inclusion Unit.

Fonagy, P., Steele, H., Steele, M., Higgitt, A. and Target, M. (1994) 'The theory and practice of resilience. The Emanuel Miller Memorial Lecture 1992.' *Journal of Child Psychology and Psychiatry 35*, 2, 231–257.

Fonagy, P., Target, M., Cottrell, D., Phillips, J. and Kurtz, Z. (2002) *What Works for Whom? A Critical Review of Treatments for Children and Adolescents.* New York and London: Guilford Press.

Food Standards Agency (2006) *FSA Nutrient and Food Based Guidelines for UK Institutions.* Available at www.food.gov.uk/multimedia/pdfs/nutguideuk.pdf, accessed 1 September 2008.

Harrison, J. and Wolley, M. (2004) *Debt and Disability: The Impact of Debt on Families with Disabled Children.* York: Contact a Family & Family Fund.

Hart, A., Blincow, D. with Thomas, H. (2007) *Resilient Therapy: Working with Children and Families.* London: Routledge.

Kohlberg, L. (1984) *The Psychology of Moral Development: The Nature and Validity of Moral Stages.* (Vol.2). New York: Harper & Row.

Layard, R. (2005) *Happiness: Lessons from a New Science.* London: Penguin.

Mackett, R.L. (2004) *Making Children's Lives More Active.* Factsheet. London: Centre for Transport Studies, University College London. Available at the website of UCL Civil, Environmental & Geomatic Engineering, www2.cege.ucl.ac.uk/cts, accessed 1 September 2008.

Marchant, R. (2008) 'Working with Disabled Children Who Live Away from Home.' In B. Luckock and M. Lefevre (eds) *Direct Work: Social Work with Children and Young People in Care.* London: BAAF.

Masten, A.S. (2001) 'Ordinary magic: Resilience processes in development.' *American Psychologist 56*, 3, 227–238.

McAfee Brown, R. (ed.) (1987) *The Essential Reinhold Niebuhr: Selected Essays and Addresses.* London and New Haven: Yale University Press.

Middleton, L. (1999) *Disabled Children: Challenging Social Exclusion.* Oxford: Blackwell.

Mind (2007) *Ecotherapy: The Green Agenda for Mental Health.* London: Mind Publications. Available at www.mind.org.uk/NR/rdonlyres/ D9A930D2-30D4-4E5B-BE79-1D401B804165/0/ecotherapy.pdf, accessed 1 September 2008.

Murray, P. (2002) *Hello! Are You Listening? Disabled Teenagers' Experience of Access to Inclusive Leisure.* Available at www.jrf.org.uk/knowledge/findings/ socialcare/pdf/712.pdf, accessed 10 November 2008.

Mussen, P.H. (ed.) (1983) *Handbook of Child Psychology. Vol. 1: History, Theory and Methods.* 4th edn. New York: Wiley.

Office of National Statistics (ONS) (2005) *The Time Use Survey – How We Spend Our Time.* Available at www.statistics.gov.uk, accessed 10 November 2008.

Oldman, C. and Beresford, B. (2002) *Homes Unfit for Children: Housing, Disabled Children and their Families.* Bristol: Policy Press.

Priestley, M. (1998) 'Childhood disability and disabled childhoods: Agendas for research.' *Childhood: A Global Journal of Childhood Research 5*, 2, 207–223.

Roisman, G.I., Padrón, E., Sroufe, L.A. and Engeland, B. (2002) 'Earned-secure attachment status in retrospect and prospect.' *Child Development 73*, 4, 1204–1219.

Russell, P. (2003) *Bridging the Gap: Developing Policy and Practice in Child Care Options for Disabled Children and their Families.* London: Council for Disabled Children.

Rutter, M. (1989) 'Isle of Wight revisited: Twenty-five years of child psychiatric epidemiology.' *Journal of the American Academy of Child & Adolescent Psychiatry 28*, 5, 633–653.

Rutter, M. (1999) 'Resilience concepts and findings: Implications for family therapy.' *Journal of Family Therapy 21*, 119–144.

Seligman, M.E.P. (2006) *Learned Optimism: How to Change Your Mind and Your Life.* New York: Vintage Books.

Shakespeare, T. (2006) *Disability Rights and Wrongs.* London: Routledge.

SIRC (2007) *Belonging.* Oxford: Issues Research Centre. Available at www.sirc.org/publik/ belonging.shtml, accessed 1 September 2008.

Ungar, M. (2005) 'Resilience among children in child welfare, corrections, mental health and educational settings: Recommendations for service.' *Child and Youth Care Forum 34*, 6, 445–463.

Winnicott, D.W. (1958) *Collected Papers: Through Paediatrics to Psycho-Analysis.* London: Tavistock.

Zealey, C. (2005) 'The benefits of infant massage: A critical review.' *Community Practitioner 78*, 3, 98–102.

RESOURCES

Books

Allen, P. (2007) *Resources for Learning Mentors: Practical Activities for Group Sessions.* London: Paul Chapman Publishing.

Altiero, J. (2007) *No More Stinking Thinking: A Workbook for Teaching Children Positive Thinking.* London and Philadelphia: Jessica Kingsley Publishers.

Brooks, R. and Goldstein, S. (2001) *Raising Resilient Children.* New York: McGraw-Hill. Available at www.drrobertbrooks.com (accessed 1 September 2008).

Brunskill, K. (2006) *Promoting Children's Resilience and Wellbeing.* Thousand Oaks and London: Paul Chapman Publishing.

Daniel, B. and Wassell, S. (2002) *The School Years: Assessing and Promoting Resilience in Vulnerable Children.* London and Philadelphia: Jessica Kingsley Publishers.

Plummer, D. (2007) *Helping Children to Build Self-Esteem: A Photocopiable Activities Book,* 2nd edn. London and Philadelphia: Jessica Kingsley Publishers.

Stallard, P. (2002) *Think Good – Feel Good: A Cognitive Behaviour Therapy Workbook for Children and Young People.* Chichester: John Wiley and Sons.

Websites and organizations

Amaze. Amaze produce a series of useful factsheets that can be downloaded. See links to Resources through the Amaze website, available at www.amazebrighton.org.uk (accessed 1 September 2008).

APA Help Center. The American Psychological Association's Help Center has some useful guides about building resilience for parents and teachers. Available at www.apahelpcenter.org/featuredtopics/feature.php?id=39 (accessed 10 November 2008).

Bouncing Back, Community University Partnership Project (CUPP) at the University of Brighton, England available at www.brighton.ac.uk/cupp/coastalcommunities/bouncingback.html, (accessed 10 Novemeber 2008).

Centre for Confidence and Well-being. The Centre for Confidence and Well-being is based in Glasgow and their website has a whole section on resilience under the Positive Psychology Resources section. Available at www.centreforconfidence.co.uk/pp/overview.php?p=c2lkPTU= (accessed 10 November 2008).

Contact a Family (CAF). CAF is a UK-wide charity providing advice, information and support to parents of disabled children. They produce a useful statistical factsheet, available at www.cafamily.org.uk/students.html (accessed 1 September 2008).

Mencap. See their resources on bullying, available at www.mencap.org.uk. (accessed 1 September 2008).

Michael Ungar is a Professor at the School of Social Work, Dalhousie University, Canada, and is an internationally recognized researcher on the subject of resilience. His website includes information about research projects including the International Resilience Project and the Pathways to Resilience Project and it has a page especially written for parents. Available at www.michaelungar.com (accessed 10 November 2008).

National Autistic Society (NAS). Their resources are available at www.autism.org.uk (accessed 1 September 2008).

National Center for Children in Poverty. The National Center for Children in Poverty is based at Columbia University and the website includes information about projects that focus on improving the odds for young children living in poverty. Available at http://nccp.org/publications/pub_389.html (accessed 10 November 2008).

Raising Resilient Children. Robert Brooks and Sam Goldstein's useful website includes information and strategies for raising children such as the resilient mindset quiz for parents. It advertises lots of books and audio materials that you can buy, but some of the information is downloadable for free. Available at www.raisingresilientkids.com/index.html (accessed 10 November 2008).

ResilienceNet Virtual Library. ResilienceNet's website includes a collection of full-text publications that you can download. Most are about research findings related to resilience and children and families. Available at www.resilnet.uiuc.edu/library.html (accessed 10 November 2008).

Resiliency Resource Centre. The Resiliency Resource Centre is based in Australia and its website provides information and tips for parents and teachers about how to promote resilience. Available at www.embracethefuture.org.au/resiliency/index.htm?http://www.embracethefuture.org.au/resiliency/what_schools_can_do.htm (accessed 10 November 2008).

INDEX

Rec
MAY 2012 **DATE DUE**

JAN 3 0 2013			
♥ REMEMBER ♥		OCT 1 4 2013	